Waynesburg College Library
Waynesburg, Pa. 15370

378.761   W317t
Washington, Booker Taliaferra
Tuskegee and its people
116081

BOOKER T. WASHINGTON.

TUSKEGEE &
ITS PEOPLE: THEIR IDEALS AND ACHIEVEMENTS

EDITED BY
BOOKER T. WASHINGTON

NEGRO UNIVERSITIES PRESS
NEW YORK

Originally published in 1905
by D. Appleton and Co.

Reprinted 1969 by
Negro Universities Press
A DIVISION OF GREENWOOD PUBLISHING CORP.
NEW YORK

SBN 8371-1423-3

PRINTED IN UNITED STATES OF AMERICA

PREFACE

In a general way the reading public is fairly well acquainted with the work of the Tuskegee Normal and Industrial Institute, but there is continued demand for definite information as to just what the graduates of that institution are doing with their education.

That inquiry is partly answered by this book. The scope of the Tuskegee Institute work is outlined by the chapters contained in Part I, while those of Part II evidence the fact that the graduates of the school are grappling at first-hand with the conditions that environ the masses of the Negro people.

At the school, in addition to the regular Normal School course of academic work, thirty-six industries are taught the young men and women. These are: Agriculture; Basketry; Blacksmithing; Bee-keeping; Brickmasonry; Plastering; Brickmaking; Carpentry; Carriage Trimming; Cooking; Dairying; Architectural, Freehand, and Me-

PREFACE

chanical Drawing; Dressmaking; Electrical and Steam Engineering; Founding; Harness-making; Housekeeping; Horticulture; Canning; Plain Sewing; Laundering; Machinery; Mattress-making; Millinery; Nurse Training; Painting; Sawmilling; Shoemaking; Printing; Stock-raising; Tailoring; Tinning; and Wheelwrighting.

Since the founding of the institution, July 4, 1881, seven hundred and forty-six graduates have gone out from the institution, while more than six thousand others who were not able to remain and complete the academic course, and thereby secure a diploma, have been influenced for good by it.

The school has sought from the very beginning to make itself of practical value to the Negro people and to the South as well. It has taught those industries that are of the South, the occupations in which our men and women find most ready employment, and unflinchingly has refused to abandon its course; it has sought to influence its young men and women to live unselfish, sacrificing lives; to put into practise the lessons taught on every side that make for practical, helpful every-day living.

In the main those who go out from Tuskegee Institute, (1) follow the industry they have been taught, (2) teach in a public or private school or

PREFACE

teach part of the year and farm or labor the rest, (3) follow housekeeping or other domestic service, or (4) enter a profession or the Government service, or become merchants. Among the teachers are many who instruct in farming or some industry; the professional men are largely physicians, and the professional women mostly trained nurses. Dr. Washington, the Principal of the school, makes the unqualified statement: "After diligent investigation, I can not find a dozen former students in idleness. They are in shop, field, schoolroom, home, or the church. They are busy because they have placed themselves in demand by learning to do that which the world wants done, and because they have learned the disgrace of idleness and the sweetness of labor."

No attempt has here been made to represent all of the industries; no attempt has especially been made to confine representation to those who are working at manual labor. The public, or at least a part of it, somewhat gratuitously, has reached the conclusion that Tuskegee Institute is a "servant training school," or an employment agency. That is a mistaken idea.

The object of the school is to train men and women who will go out and repeat the work done

PREFACE

here, to teach what they have learned to others, and to leaven the whole mass of the Negro people in the South with a desire for the knowledge and profitable operation of those industries in which they have in so large a measure the right of way. Tuskegee students and graduates are never urged not to take such service, especially not to refuse in preference to idleness, but it all involves a simple, ordinary, economic principle. Capable men and women, skilled in the industrial arts, are like those of all races—they seek the most profitable employment. A blacksmith, a tailor, a brickmason, a harness-maker, or other artisan, who can find work in shops and factories, or independently, and make thirty to seventy-five dollars a month, and even more, will not, simply because he is black, leave those chances to accept service in private employment for fifteen dollars per month, and less, and board himself. No school could covenant to train servants for an indefinite tenure; it can at best only promise to train leaders who shall go among the masses and lift them up; to train men and women who shall in turn reach hundreds of others.

Those who write the following chapters represent, in the main, this class. They have written simply, with perfect frankness, have dealt with the

PREFACE

significant things of their lives, and have demonstrated, the writer believes, that from humble origin black men and women may confidently be counted upon, with proper encouragement, to win success. The chapters are autobiographical, significantly optimistic, with just pride in what has been done, and outlining, as did " Up from Slavery"—which was commended as a proper model—experiences from childhood, the school-life of the writer, and the results achieved in the direction of putting into practise what was learned in school. Through this symposium it is hoped that the public may learn, in the best possible way, some of the finer results already accomplished by the Tuskegee Institute.

E. J. S.

Tuskegee Institute, Alabama, *April 1, 1905.*

CONTENTS

	PAGE
GENERAL INTRODUCTION	1
By Booker T. Washington.	

PART I

THE SCHOOL AND ITS PURPOSES

I.—PRESENT ACHIEVEMENTS AND GOVERNING IDEALS 19
By Emmett J. Scott, Mr. Washington's Executive Secretary.

II.—RESOURCES AND MATERIAL EQUIPMENT . . 35
By Warren Logan, Treasurer of the School.

III.—THE ACADEMIC AIMS 56
By Roscoe C. Bruce, Director of the Academic Department.

IV.—WHAT GIRLS ARE TAUGHT, AND HOW . . . 68
By Mrs. Booker T. Washington, Director of Industries for Girls.

V.—HAMPTON INSTITUTE'S RELATION TO TUSKEGEE 87
By Robert R. Moton.

PART II

AUTOBIOGRAPHIES BY GRADUATES OF THE SCHOOL

I.—A COLLEGE PRESIDENT'S STORY 101
By Isaac Fisher, of Pine Bluff, Arkansas.

II.—A SCHOOL PRINCIPAL'S STORY 111
By William H. Holtzclaw, of Utica, Mississippi.

CONTENTS

	PAGE
III.—A LAWYER'S STORY	141

By George W. Lovejoy, of Mobile, Alabama.

IV.—A SCHOOL TREASURER'S STORY 152
By Martin A. Menafee, of Denmark, South Carolina.

V.—THE STORY OF A FARMER 164
By Frank Reid, of Dawkins, Alabama.

VI.—THE STORY OF A CARPENTER . . . 173
By Gabriel B. Miller, of Fort Valley, Georgia.

VII.—COTTON-GROWING IN AFRICA 184
By John W. Robinson, of Lome, Togo, West Africa.

VIII.—THE STORY OF A TEACHER OF COOKING . 200
By Mary L. Dotson, of Tuskegee Institue, Alabama.

IX.—A WOMAN'S WORK 211
By Cornelia Bowen, of Waugh (Mt. Meigs), Alabama.

X.—UPLIFTING OF THE SUBMERGED MASSES . 224
By W. J. Edwards, of Snow Hill, Alabama.

XI.—A DAIRYMAN'S STORY 253
By Lewis A. Smith, of Rockford, Illinois.

XII.—THE STORY OF A WHEELWRIGHT . . . 264
By Edward Lomax, of Tuskegee Institute, Alabama.

XIII.—THE STORY OF A BLACKSMITH 276
By Jubie B. Bragg, of Tallahassee, Florida.

XIV.—A DRUGGIST'S STORY 285
By David L. Johnston, of Birmingham, Alabama.

XV.—THE STORY OF A SUPERVISOR OF MECHAN-
ICAL INDUSTRIES 299
By James M. Canty, of Institute P. O., West Virginia.

XVI.—A NEGRO COMMUNITY BUILDER 317
By Russell C. Calhoun, of Eatonville, Florida.

XVII.—THE EVOLUTION OF A SHOEMAKER . . . 338
By Charles L. Marshall, of Cambria, Virginia.

LIST OF ILLUSTRATIONS

                                                  FACING PAGE

BOOKER T. WASHINGTON . . . . *Frontispiece*

EMMETT J. SCOTT 20
    Mr. Washington's Executive Secretary.

THE COLLIS P. HUNTINGTON MEMORIAL BUILDING 26

WARREN LOGAN 36
    Treasurer of the School

THE OFFICE BUILDING IN PROCESS OF ERECTION . 50
    Student carpenters shown at work.

ROSCOE C. BRUCE 56
    Director of the Academic Department.

A PORTION OF THE SCHOOL GROUNDS 64

ANOTHER PORTION OF THE SCHOOL GROUNDS . . 66

MRS. BOOKER T. WASHINGTON 68
    Director of Industries for Girls.

A CLASS IN MILLINERY 76

THE EXECUTIVE COUNCIL 94
    Standing, left to right: P. C. Parks, Superintendent of Farm; George W. Carver, Director, Agricultural Department; J. N. Calloway, Land Extension; John H. Palmer, Registrar; Charles H. Gibson, Resident Auditor; Edgar J. Penney, Chaplain.
    Seated, left to right: Lloyd G. Wheeler, Business Agent; Robert R. Taylor, Director of Mechanical Industries; John H. Washington, General Superintendent of Industries; Warren Logan, Treasurer; Booker T. Washington, Principal; Miss Jane E. Clark, Dean of Woman's Department; Mrs. Booker T. Washington, Director of Industries for Girls; and Emmett J. Scott, Secretary to the Principal.
    The Director of the Academic Department, Roscoe C. Bruce, and the Commandant of Cadets, Major J. B. Ramsey, also members of the Executive Council, were absent when photograph was taken.

LIST OF ILLUSTRATIONS

	FACING PAGE
THE CARNEGIE LIBRARY BUILDING	108
MORNING AT THE BARNS ON THE SCHOOL FARM	122
Teams of horses and cattle ready to start for the day's work.	
STUDENTS PRUNING PEACH-TREES	146
A SILO ON THE FARM	166
Students filling it with fodder corn, steam-power being used.	
A MODEL DINING-ROOM	208
From the department where table-service is taught.	
THE CULTURE OF BEES	220
Students at work in the apiary.	
IN THE DAIRY	254
Students using separators.	
STUDENTS AT WORK IN THE HARNESS SHOP	270
AT THE HOSPITAL	294
A corner in the boys' ward.	
IN THE TIN SHOP	300
STUDENTS CANNING FRUIT	308
STARTING A NEW BUILDING	314
Student masons laying the foundation in brick.	
GIRLS GARDENING	344

TUSKEGEE AND ITS PEOPLE

GENERAL INTRODUCTION

By Booker T. Washington

INSTITUTIONS, like individuals, are properly judged by their ideals, their methods, and their achievements in the production of men and women who are to do the world's work.

One school is better than another in proportion as its system touches the more pressing needs of the people it aims to serve, and provides the more speedily and satisfactorily the elements that bring to them honorable and enduring success in the struggle of life. Education of some kind is the first essential of the young man, or young woman, who would lay the foundation of a career. The choice of the school to which one will go and the calling he will adopt must be influenced in a very large measure by his environments, trend of ambition, natural capacity, possible opportunities

TUSKEGEE AND ITS PEOPLE

in the proposed calling, and the means at his command.

In the past twenty-four years thousands of the youth of this and other lands have elected to come to the Tuskegee Normal and Industrial Institute to secure what they deem the training that would offer them the widest range of usefulness in the activities open to the masses of the Negro people. Their hopes, fears, strength, weaknesses, struggles, and triumphs can not fail to be of absorbing interest to the great body of American people, more particularly to the student of educational theories and their attendant results.

When an institution has, like Tuskegee Institute, reached that stage in its development that its system of instruction has aroused very general discussion, and has given to the world of varied industry an army of workers, numbering not less than 6,000, there is a natural curiosity on the part of the public to learn all that is possible of such an institution, and of the personality and methods of those administering its affairs. They wish to ascertain the actual truth concerning its resources and equipment; they want figures detailing the degree of pecuniary productiveness and moral efficiency attained by those who have re-

GENERAL INTRODUCTION

ceived the prescribed training; and they are eager to hear the whole story from the lips of both the instructors and the instructed as to how the recorded results have been accomplished.

In several volumes already published, bearing upon Tuskegee Institute and what it stands for, an endeavor has been made to present a truthful account of the Principal's early strivings and lifework; an honest attempt has been made to analyze and impress the basic principles upon which Tuskegee Institute was founded. It has been the aim to write a history of individual yearnings for the light of knowledge that would stir the inner consciousness of the humblest of the race and arouse him to the vast possibilities that lie in the wake of solid character, intelligent industry, and material acquisition. He has tried, with all earnestness, to hold up the future of the American Negro in its most attractive aspect, and to emphasize the virile philosophy that there is a positive dignity in working with the hands, when that labor is fortified by a developed brain and a consecrated heart.

Though much has been said of the spirit and purpose of this center of social and economic uplift in the famed Black Belt of the South, there is still a wide-spread demand for a more specific

TUSKEGEE AND ITS PEOPLE

recital of what is being done here, by whom, under what conditions, and the concrete evidences of the benefits that are growing out of the thrift, industry, right thinking, and right living taught by our faculty.

In response to this insistent call, Mr. Emmett J. Scott, Executive Secretary of the Tuskegee Institute, presents to the public a further contribution, Tuskegee and Its People: Their Ideals and Achievements, with authentic accompanying autobiographies of a number of typical students of the school.

To this work Mr. Scott brings a peculiar fitness, unequaled by any other person who might have been chosen to perform it. He is closely knit to the Southland and her great masses by the common sympathy of nativity and the mutuality of hopes. The South has always been his home, but he has traveled so extensively and mingled so freely that he has acquired most ample breadth of vision as regards men and things.

For many years now Mr. Scott has served the school with rare fidelity and zeal, and has been to the Principal not only a loyal assistant in every phase of his manifold and frequently trying duties, but has proved a valuable personal friend and

GENERAL INTRODUCTION

counselor in matters of the most delicate nature, exhibiting in emergencies a quality of judgment and diplomatic calmness seldom found in men of even riper maturity and more extended experience.

As I stated in one of my books published several years ago, as far as one individual can fill the place of another, Mr. Scott has acted in the Principal's stead, seeing with the Principal's eyes and hearing with the Principal's ears, counting no sacrifice too great to be made for Tuskegee's well-being. He is in perfect accord with the fundamental principles and practical policies through the persistent adherence to which Tuskegee Institute has won its conspicuous place in the educational world.

The volume here presented has been edited by Mr. Scott with the utmost care, he preferring to have the contributors understate rather than overstate the results that have come from the labors of Tuskegee and its people. It has been the Principal's pleasure and privilege to examine and critically review the manuscript after its completion, and the volume is so praiseworthy that it is given his cordial approval. The task of editing he had expected to perform has been so well done that it has only been necessary to review the manuscript after its preparation for the publishers, and to forego the strict editorial revisioning planned. The book is an accurate portrait of the Tuskegee of to-day, and reasonably forecasts the hopes for the institution of to-morrow. It tells with forceful directness and graphic precision the formative work that is being done for this generation, and supplies a fulcrum upon which there may justly rest a prophecy of greater things for the generations that are to follow.

A Tuskegee book, whatever its primary motive, is invariably expected to deal broadly with the entire problem of the Negro and his relationships of every kind. It must be more than a mere flesh-and-blood narrative, descriptive of the material progress of the men and women the Institute has produced and is producing. It must be a book free from ostentatious pretension, breathing the atmosphere of the life of the earnest people it describes. It must, of course, exhibit not only the achievements, but also the ideals, the possibilities of the Tuskegee trained man and woman. This, I feel, is adequately done in this volume.

Tuskegee and Its People possesses ideals in thought, morals, and action—and they are lofty. In these respects the symposium will not prove a

GENERAL INTRODUCTION

disappointment. This instinct for the ideal, however, lies not in idly sighing for it, but is born of an abiding belief that worth is intrinsic, and that applied common sense, practical knowledge, constancy of effort, and mechanical skill will make a place for the patient striver far more secure than the artificial niche into which some one may thrust him. The masses who are most helpfully reached by the Tuskegee Institute are coming to realize that education in its truest sense is no longer to be regarded as an emotional impulse, a fetish made up of loosely joined information, to be worshiped for its mere possession, but as a practical means to a definite end. They are being taught that mind-training is the logical helpmeet of hand-training, and that both, supplemented and sweetened by heart-training, make the high-souled, useful, productive, patriotic, law-loving, public-spirited citizen, of whom any nation might well be proud. The outcome of such education will be that, instead of the downtrodden child of ignorance, shiftlessness, and moral weakness, we shall generate the thoroughly rounded man of prudence, foresight, responsibility, and financial independence. He will cease to be the gullible victim of the sharper who plays upon vanity, credulity,

TUSKEGEE AND ITS PEOPLE

and superstition, and learn to value only that which is real and substantial. It is of the highest importance to the Negro, who must make his way amid disadvantages and embarrassments of the severest character, that he be made aware of the vast difference between working and being worked. In carrying this inspiring message and impressing these fundamental truths, the new Tuskegee book renders a splendid service.

Industrial training will be more potent for good to the race when its relation to the other phases of essential education is more clearly understood. There is afloat no end of discussion as to what is the "proper kind of education for the Negro," and much of it is hurtful to the cause it is designed to promote. The danger, at present, that most seriously threatens the success of industrial training, is the ill-advised insistence in certain quarters that this form of education should be offered to the exclusion of all other branches of knowledge. If the idea becomes fixed in the minds of the people that industrial education means class education, that it should be offered the Negro because he is a Negro, and that the Negro should be confined to this sort of education, then I fear serious injury will be done the cause of hand-train-

GENERAL INTRODUCTION

ing. It should be understood rather that at such institutions as Hampton Institute and Tuskegee Institute, industrial education is not emphasized because colored people are to receive it, but because the ripest educational thought of the world approves it; because the undeveloped material resources of the South make it peculiarly important for both races; and because it should be given in a large measure to any race, regardless of color, which is in the same stage of development as the Negro.

On the other hand, no one understanding the real needs of the race would advocate that industrial education should be given to every Negro to the exclusion of the professions and other branches of learning. It is evident that a race so largely segregated as the Negro is, must have an increasing number of its own professional men and women. There is, then, a place and an increasing need for the Negro college as well as for the industrial institute, and the two classes of schools should, and as a matter of fact do, cooperate in the common purpose of elevating the masses. There is nothing in hand-training to suggest that it is a class-training. The best educational authorities in the world are indorsing it as an essential feature in the education of both races, and especially so when a very large proportion of the people in question are compelled by dint of circumstances to earn their living in manufactures and agricultural and mechanical pursuits in general. It so happens that the bulk of our people are permanently to remain in the South, and conditions beyond their control have attached them to the soil; for a long time the status of the majority of them is likely to be that of laborers. To make hard conditions easier, to raise common labor from drudgery to dignity, and to adopt systems of training that will meet the needs of the greatest number and prepare them for the better things that intelligent effort will surely bring, form a task to which the wisest of the race are addressing themselves with an eager enthusiasm which refuses to be chilled by adverse criticism.

Tuskegee emphasizes industrial training for the Negro, not with the thought that the Negro should be confined to industrialism, the plow, or the hoe, but because the undeveloped material resources of the South offer at this time a field peculiarly advantageous to the worker skilled in agriculture and the industries, and here are found the Negro's most inviting opportunities for taking on

GENERAL INTRODUCTION

the rudimentary elements that ultimately make for a permanently progressive civilization.

The Tuskegee Idea is that correct education begins at the bottom, and expands naturally as the necessities of the people expand. As the race grows in knowledge, experience, culture, taste, and wealth, its wants are bound to become more and more diverse; and to satisfy these wants there will be gradually developed within our own ranks—as has already been true of the whites—a constantly increasing variety of professional and business men and women. Their places in the economic world will be assured and their prosperity guaranteed in proportion to the merit displayed by them in their several callings, for about them will have been established the solid bulwark of an industrial mass to which they may safely look for support. The esthetic demands will be met as the capacity of the race to procure them is enlarged through the processes of sane intellectual advancement. In this cumulative way there will be erected by the Negro, and for the Negro, a complete and indestructible civilization that will be respected by all whose respect is worth the having. There should be no limit placed upon the development of any individual because of color, and let it be understood that no one kind of training can safely be prescribed for any entire race. Care should be taken that racial education be not one-sided for lack of adaptation to person fitness, nor unwieldy through sheer top-heaviness. Education, to fulfil its mission for any people anywhere, should be symmetrical and sensible.

A mastery of the industries taught at Tuskegee presupposes and requires no small degree of academic study, for competency in agriculture calls for considerable knowledge of chemistry, and no mechanical pursuit can be followed satisfactorily without some acquaintance with mathematics and the "three R's." Likewise, the individual of liberal academic or college preparation possesses a stronger equipment for constructive work who has trained his hands to supplement his brain.

After all, the final test of the value of any system of education is found in the record of its actual achievements. In Tuskegee and Its People heads of the several departments have not only given a succinct account of the history, resources, and current labors of the school, but deal most happily with the governing ideals behind the institution, and vindicate its claim to the approval of the world's thinkers and moving forces. Besides

GENERAL INTRODUCTION

treating rather elaborately the structural efficiency of the work of the teachers, the editor has not neglected to emphasize the spiritual and ethical virtues that spread over a wider range of influence here and among our people throughout the Southland than those familiar with the purely academic phases have adequately understood.

Tuskegee's germ principle is to be found in its unboasted ideals, in the things that of necessity can not be listed in catalogue or report, rather than in its buildings, shops, farms, and what not. The school dwells upon the saving power of land, and learning, and skill, and a bank-account—not as finalities in themselves, but as tangible witnesses to the Negro's capacity to compete with others.

Perhaps the newest and most refreshing feature of the book is its vivid pen-portraits of the young men and women who have gone out of Tuskegee carrying into diversified lives the principles and precepts imbibed from their parent school. The pictures are drawn by the originals themselves, and they illustrate by honorable achievement the wholesome and evangelizing influence of Tuskegee's preachments, and the far-reaching effect of placing before them as teachers the highest example of what the Negro of morals and manners may become. They tell their story at first-hand, modestly and sincerely, and the foundations of inspiring lives, laid in the Christian virtues and conscientious service of their fellow men, foster a firm belief that the school is doing a work that will live.

These types of Tuskegee's graduates, picked out at random from hundreds of equal scholarship and ability, represent distinctive channels of activity, including the president of a leading college, principals and teachers of thriving schools, a lawyer, a tinner, a school treasurer, farmers, cotton-growers, master builders and contractors, a dairyman, and a blacksmith. No element contributing to the racial uplift is overlooked. The scenes of their labors are scattered over a vast area, showing convincingly the diffusive character as well as the rich harvest garnered through the Tuskegee Idea. These rough-hewn sketches of a sturdy pioneer band in staking out a larger life and a wider horizon for later generations are worthy of the most careful perusal.

The immeasurable advancement of the Negro, manifested in character, courage, and cash, vitalized by valiant service to the republic in education, commerce, and religion, and crowned by an

GENERAL INTRODUCTION

enlightened, vigorously efficient, sensibly ambitious, and law-abiding citizenship, is "confirmation strong as proofs of Holy Writ" that the gospel of industry, as exemplified by Tuskegee and its helpers, has exerted a leavening influence upon civilization wherever it has been brought within the reach of those who are struggling toward the heights. Under this new dispensation of mind, morals, and muscle, with the best whites and best blacks in sympathetic cooperation, and justice meaning the same to the weak as to the strong, the South will no longer be vexed by a "race problem." Peace and prosperity for all will come with the strength to rise above the baser self. Civic righteousness is the South's speediest thoroughfare to economic greatness.

A book that opens the inner chambers of a people's heart, and sheds a light that may guide the footsteps of both races along the upward way, should meet with a hearty welcome at the hands of all lovers of mankind.

PART I
THE SCHOOL AND ITS PURPOSES

I

PRESENT ACHIEVEMENTS AND GOVERNING IDEALS

By Emmett J. Scott

So much has been said about Tuskegee Institute as a training-school in which to prepare young colored men and women for earning a living in the world of trade and business, that the ideals and spirit behind all this training are to a very large extent lost sight of.

Tuskegee, with its hundreds of acres of farm-land under intelligent cultivation, with its ever-increasing number of well-appointed buildings and its equipment, and the many things on the grounds included in the name of handicrafts, is always in the public eye, and continually appeals to the interest of those who are deeply concerned in the well-being and progress of the Negro people.

Yet behind all of these more tangible manifestations of work, skill, and achievement, there is an unseen, persistent groping after the higher ideals of life and living. No one can remain long on the grounds as an intelligent observer of all that is to be here seen and felt, without recognizing that the things that are not written in the catalogue and not a part of the daily program of activities are real, vital, and of far-reaching importance.

Principal Booker T. Washington and the men and women who have helped him to build Tuskegee Institute are constantly looking beyond the present to a future filled with the evidences of a better living for all those who have felt the transforming spirit of the hidden forces at work.

How the perspective widens and deepens! Far, far beyond the confines of the Tuskegee Institute community the light of this new life is seen and felt and has its salutary effect. The stagnant life of centuries has awakened, and is casting off its bonds. A new term, "intelligent thrift," has come into its possession. Wherever this term has gone and taken root, there has gone with it the thought that unless the idea make for character, as well as for more cotton or corn, it is not of much value.

The Tuskegee Idea always asks one question, and that is, "What are you?" and not, "What have you?" The man who does not rise superior to his possessions does not measure up to the Tuskegee idea of manhood.

EMMETT J. SCOTT.
Mr. Washington's Executive Secretary.

PRESENT ACHIEVEMENTS

In other words, character-building is the Alpha and Omega of all that Tuskegee stands for. From the moment the new student comes on the grounds until he leaves, he is appealed to in ways innumerable to regard life as more than bread or meat, as more than mere mental equipment. Cleanliness, decorum, promptness, truthfulness—these are old-fashioned virtues, and are more properly taught in the home, but in Tuskegee they mean everything. Tuskegee not only acts as a teacher, but assumes the rôle of parent, and lays emphasis on the importance of these virtues every moment of the time from the entrance of the student until Commencement Day. The " cleanliness that is next to godliness " is one of the Tuskegee ideals, and a student can scarcely commit a more serious misdemeanor than to appear slovenly, either in dress or manners. The facilities and requirements for bathing are quite as complete and exacting as the equipments in the laboratories and recitation-rooms. The result is that Tuskegee has the reputation of being one of the most cleanly and sanitary institutions in the South.

As for good manners, Lord Chesterfield himself would scarcely ask more than is insisted upon by Tuskegee precision. A man must first be conscious of being a gentleman before he can be recognized as such by others, and a girl's good manners are only outward evidences of her individual worth and passport to respectful treatment. Tuskegee Institute, then, insists upon these things because they make for character, and are a part of the ideals toward which all training tends.

But how are all these things taught and enforced? The first requisite, of course, is the character of the teachers and instructors themselves, the men and women who are the embodiment of the ideals that Tuskegee Institute stands for. While it can not be claimed that the best teachers in the South are all at Tuskegee, it can be said that no other school has so large a number of colored men and women who have had the advantage of the highest industrial and intellectual, moral and religious training. The teaching force is made up largely of graduates from nearly every first-class educational institution in America. These teachers have been carefully sought out and brought to Tuskegee, not only for their teaching ability, but that the students may have the benefit of the best examples before them of what the highest culture can do for men and women of their own race. For the majority of our students the perspective of life is

PRESENT ACHIEVEMENTS

narrow: many of them have never lived out of the community in which they were born. That was their only world; their ideals of life were shaped by their mean and narrow environments. They have learned to believe, and act accordingly, that the best people are all of one complexion, and the worst and poorest people are all of another complexion. There is no such thing as creating a sentiment of race pride in such people unless they have set before them living examples of their own race in whom they can feel a sense of pride.

It is scarcely too much to say that one of the best things about the Tuskegee Institute is that it wins our young men and women from mean and sordid environment and brings them in contact with teachers whose minds, hearts, and lives have been enlarged and graced by the highest learning in the best educational institutions of the country. The school teaches no more important lesson than that of cultivating a sense of pride and respect for colored men and women who deserve it because of their character, education, and achievements.

Pride of race, though not so written in the courses of study, is as much a part of Tuskegee's work as agriculture, brick-making, millinery, or any other trade, and quite as important. This may

TUSKEGEE AND ITS PEOPLE

be called sentiment, but it makes for race development quite as much as any of the material things taught in the class-room or shop. To borrow a line from George Eliot:

> "Because our race has no great memories,
> I will so live, it shall remember me
> For deeds of such divine beneficence
> As rivers have, that teach men what is good
> By blessing them—
> And make their name, now but a badge of scorn,
> A glorious banner floating in their midst,
> Stirring the air they breathe with impulses
> Of generous pride, exalting fellowship
> Until it soars to magnanimity."

That self-respect demands race pride; that virtue is its own reward; that character is the greatest thing in human life, are taught and emphasized in other ways also. Dr. Washington has succeeded, to a remarkable degree, in developing the Tuskegee Institute by insisting that this institution must have nothing less than the best within and without it, everywhere. What is not best is only temporary. Those who have done most for the school have been made to feel that the character of the work done here and the ideals striven for are deserving of the best. The idea that " anything is good enough for a Negro school " has never been allowed to have

PRESENT ACHIEVEMENTS

any part or exert any effect in Tuskegee's expansion.

For example, when Mr. Carnegie donated the money for a library for Tuskegee, a building was erected of classic outline—a noble structure of artistic symmetry and beauty that must appeal to every one who has any appreciation of architectural beauty. The Collis P. Huntington Memorial Building, just completed, a gift of Mrs. C. P. Huntington, used for the academic classes of the school, would be a credit and delight to any municipality. There is everything about the exterior and interior that must awaken a sense of pride in every pupil who enters its portals. Its facilities are sensible and unostentatious, yet they meet every requirement of the department. What is true of the new Academic Building is likewise true of the various dormitories for girls and boys. The cleanliness and the sanitation to be found at Tuskegee are in delightful contrast to the poor environment to which many of the students have been accustomed; especially is this contrast heightened when these same students have, under competent direction, installed the plants which yield these comforts. Thus it is that in dormitory, recitation-room, shop, dining-hall, library, chapel, and landscape, the idea that only the best is worth having and striving for is emphasized as an object-lesson and principle with such insistence that it becomes an actual part of a student's training and life.

The student at Tuskegee is constantly being trained to look up and forward. He learns how the idea of beauty can be actualized in home and social life; how faithful performance of every duty means nobility of character; how the value of achievement is determined by the motive behind it. But besides these, the one aim, thought, or anxiety around which all others revolve is the high honorableness of all kinds of work intelligently done.

In a section where those who work with their hands are marked off by the inexorable line of caste from those who work with their brains or not at all, this idea of making intelligent work more honorable than intelligent idleness is of constructive value in race development. The problem that the Tuskegee Institute is helping to solve is not only that the colored people shall do their proportionate share of the work, but that they shall do it in such a way that the benefits will remain with those who do the work. Who can measure the transforming effect and influence when it can

THE COLLIS P. HUNTINGTON MEMORIAL BUILDING.

PRESENT ACHIEVEMENTS

be said that the "best mechanics" and the "best agriculturists" in the South are Negroes? Certainly, if such a time ever comes, there will be no such painful thing as a race problem, as Negroes now see it and feel it.

This is one of Tuskegee's largest ideals; not that Tuskegee alone can bring about a "consummation so devoutly to be wished," but it is ambitious to be a potent factor in all the tendencies that make for such a condition of life in the heart of the South. So important is this aim and idea of Tuskegee, that it allows no criticism to affect, interfere, or obscure its vision. Tuskegee says to the world that it is determined not only to be a school, but an agent of civilization, a missionary for a better life, that shall stand for a kindlier relationship between the races.

The school enthusiastically seeks to live up to the ideal of its Principal, that education in the broadest and truest sense is designed to influence individuals to help others; is designed, first, last, and all the time, to transform and energize individuals into life-giving agencies for the uplift of their fellows. Principal Washington's whole educational creed, accepted by Tuskegee Institute teachers and students alike, was recently declared

TUSKEGEE AND ITS PEOPLE

in one of his familiar Sunday-evening "talks" to the students of the institution. Said he:

"Education in the broadest and truest sense will make an individual seek to help all people, regardless of race, regardless of color, regardless of condition. And you will find that the person who is most truly educated is the one who is going to be kindest, and is going to act in the gentlest manner toward persons who are unfortunate, toward the race or the individual that is most despised. The highly educated person is the one who is most considerate of those individuals who are less fortunate. I hope when you go out from here and meet persons who are afflicted by poverty, whether of mind or body, or persons who are unfortunate in any way, that you will show your education by being just as kind and considerate toward those persons as it is possible for you to be. That is the way to test a person with education. You may see ignorant persons, who perhaps think themselves educated, going about the street, and when they meet an individual who is unfortunate—lame, or with a defect of body, mind, or speech—are inclined to laugh at and make sport of that individual. But the highly educated person, the one who is really cultivated, is gentle and sympathetic

PRESENT ACHIEVEMENTS

to every one. Education is meant to make us absolutely honest in dealing with our fellows. I do not care how much arithmetic we have, or how many cities we can locate; it is all useless unless we have an education that makes us absolutely honest. Education is meant to make us give satisfaction, and to get satisfaction out of giving it. It is meant to make us get happiness out of service for our fellows. And until we get to the point where we can get happiness and supreme satisfaction out of helping our fellows, we are not truly educated. . . . Education is meant to make us appreciate the things that are beautiful in nature. A person is never educated until he is able to go into the swamps and woods and see something that is beautiful in the trees and shrubs there—is able to see something beautiful in the grass and flowers that surround him—is, in short, able to see something beautiful, elevating, and inspiring in everything that God has created. Not only should education enable us to see beauty in these objects which God has put about us, but it is meant to influence us to bring beautiful objects about us. I hope that each one of you, after you graduate, will surround himself at home with what is beautiful, inspiring, and elevating. I do not believe that any person is educated so long as he lives in a dirty, miserable shanty. I do not believe that any person is educated until he has learned to want to live in a clean room made attractive with pictures and books, and with such surroundings as are elevating. In a word, I wish to say again that education is meant to give us that culture, that refinement, that taste, which will make us deal truthfully and sympathetically with our fellow men, and will make us see what is beautiful, elevating, and inspiring in what God has created. I want you to bear in mind that your text-books, with all their contents, are not an end, but a means to an end—a means to help us get the highest, the best, the purest, and the most beautiful things out of life."

The Tuskegee trained boy or girl has set before him every hour in the day, and every day in the year, the substantial educational ideals here set forth. Books, valuable as they are, and nowhere more thoroughly reckoned as such than here, are only a means to an end: this is the gospel preached by the Tuskegee teacher. Life is the great, the eternal thing; the serving of one's fellows, the ministering unto the needy of a groping, developing people—this is the thing not forgotten, but ever constantly enforced by precept and by example.

PRESENT ACHIEVEMENTS

The many old and time-worn frame buildings are being replaced by finely built and imposing brick and stone structures; the tallow dip and antiquated oil-lamp and gas-jet, as illuminators, have paled before the more brilliant white light of electricity, installed by Tuskegee students and operated by them. Patience and faith!—these are Tuskegee's watchwords and her standard virtues. What can not be accomplished to-day will certainly be accomplished to-morrow.

So, in its larger outlook and household anxieties, Tuskegee Institute teachers are confident that the things taught and enforced by example and precept will justify their efforts in helping to make a dependent people independent, a distracted people confident, and an humble people to thrill with pride in itself and in its best men and women. Thus it is that Tuskegee Institute has never been satisfied with being merely a school, concerned wholly with its recitations and training in shop and field. Every student who carries a diploma from these grounds is urged not to hang that diploma on the wall as an ornament, as an evidence of individual superiority, but to make it mean something constructive and life-giving to every one in the community where he must live and work.

TUSKEGEE AND ITS PEOPLE

The young men and women who are trained for mission work in foreign countries are not more carefully trained in the spirit of consecration than are these young men and women trained at Tuskegee for the work of creating better economic and social conditions among their own people. It is not necessary to state here what has already been accomplished in many parts of the South by Tuskegee graduates. The selected examples set forth in this book are evidence enough. It is sufficient to say that the Tuskegee Institute is determined to become more and more a distinctive influence among the regenerative agencies that are gradually bringing order out of chaos, and justice, peace, and happiness out of the wretched disorders of a painful past. It is easy to trace the influence of such well-established institutions as Harvard and Yale in the progressive life of the American people. The sons of Harvard and Yale almost dominate civilization in America. In another sense, it is possible for Tuskegee to have a like influence in the many things that must be accomplished in the South, before love and justice shall supplant race prejudice and race antagonism.

This reaching out helpfully in all directions

PRESENT ACHIEVEMENTS

where help is needed is the distinguishing feature of Tuskegee. This race-loving spirit gives it a largeness of view and purpose that saves both its teachers and pupils from being narrow and self-centered. Take from Tuskegee all this "vision splendid," and it will at once shrink into commonplace insignificance. "Set your ideals high," says the distinguished man who here is Principal as he was founder, "and in your efforts to reach them you become strong for greater things." It is but truth to say that no institution in all the land, whether for white or black education, stands for higher and more generous ideals.

Unless the young man who goes away from Tuskegee as blacksmith, carpenter, printer, or as any other mechanic, is something more than these, he has been incapable of perceiving and taking in the ideals that go with these accomplishments. He has been taught over and over again to "hitch his wagon to the stars," and if he fail to do so, the fault is in himself, and not in Tuskegee.

As between a poor doctor and a poor carpenter, there is but scant choice. They are both failures and to be avoided. Honor in one is as precious as in the other. Honor and efficiency—these, therefore, are the ideal test of every son and daughter

TUSKEGEE AND ITS PEOPLE

that passes out of these grounds into the larger world of work and responsibility.

What a terrible task it has been and still is to teach the lessons of the upward spirit: " God's in His heaven, all's well with the world." Hope is strength and discouragement is weakness. Everything that is false and unjust and wrong is transitory. Those who are brave enough to solve problems shall be more honored of mankind than those who create problems which they make no effort to solve.

There can be no liberty without intelligence, no independence without industry, and no power for man, and no charm for woman, without character.

These are some of the ideals toward which all our teaching leads; without these there would be no Tuskegee; with them, as its very life and spirit and inspiration, Tuskegee shall lead into more ways of peace, happiness, and power than we of this generation have yet dreamed of, or realized.

II

RESOURCES AND MATERIAL EQUIPMENT

By Warren Logan

When the Alabama Legislature in 1881 passed an act to establish a Normal School for colored people at Tuskegee and appropriated for it $2,000 yearly, it made no provision whatever for land or buildings; these were left to be provided for by the people who were to be benefited by the school. Here was almost a case of being required to make bricks without straw. But as matters have turned out, this neglect was the best thing that could have happened to the school. First it gave opportunity for the employment of those splendid qualities of pluck, self-help, and perseverance which have distinguished Mr. Washington so preeminently in the building of Tuskegee. Moreover, the State has contributed nothing to the school in the way of land or buildings; it has not sought to control the property of the institution, leaving it free to be managed by the Board of Trustees.

TUSKEGEE AND ITS PEOPLE

The school was opened on the 4th of July, 1881, in an old church building in the town of Tuskegee, which lies nearly two miles from the present school-grounds. Later in the same year the growth of the school made it necessary to obtain additional room, which was found in a dilapidated shanty standing near the church and which had been used as the village schoolhouse since the war. These buildings were in such bad condition that when it rained it was necessary for the teacher and students to use umbrellas in order to protect themselves from the elements while recitations were being conducted.

Students who came from a distance boarded in families in the town, where the conditions of living were very much like those in their own homes, and these were far below proper standards. Mr. Washington, understanding the great need for colored people to be trained in correct ways of living as well as to be educated in books, determined to secure a permanent location for the school, with buildings in which the students might live under the care and influence of teachers day and night, during the whole period of their connection with the school.

It so happened at this time that there was an

WARREN LOGAN.
Treasurer of the School.

RESOURCES AND EQUIPMENT

old farm of 100 acres in the western part of the town of Tuskegee, well suited to be the site of such a school, which could be had for $500. But where was the money to be found to pay for it? Mr. Washington himself had no money, and the people of the town, much interested as they were in the enterprise, were wholly unable to give direct financial assistance. General J. F. B. Marshall, then treasurer of the Hampton Institute in Virginia, was appealed to for a loan of $200 with which to make the first payment. This he gladly made, and the farm was secured. In a few months sufficient money was raised from entertainments and subscriptions in the North and South (one friend in Connecticut giving $300) to return the loan of General Marshall and pay the balance due on the purchase of the property.

The land thus secured, preparations were at once begun to put up a school building, toward the cost of which Mr. A. H. Porter, of Brooklyn, N. Y., gave $500, the structure being named Porter Hall in recognition of Mr. Porter's generosity. In this building, which has three stories and a basement, all the operations of the school were for a time conducted. In the basement were a kitchen, dining-room, laundry, and commis-

TUSKEGEE AND ITS PEOPLE

sary. The first story was devoted to academic and industrial class-rooms; in the second was an assembly-room, where devotions and public exercises for the whole school were held, while the third was given up to dormitories.

From this small beginning has grown the present extensive plant at Tuskegee, comprising 2,300 acres of land, on which are located 123 buildings of all kinds devoted to the uses of the institution. Some idea of the impression which the size of the school makes upon one who sees it for the first time may be gathered from the remark of a Northern visitor, who, upon returning to his home from a trip through the South, was asked by a friend if he had seen "Booker Washington's school." "School?" he replied. "I have seen Booker Washington's city."

About 150 acres constitute the present campus, the rest of the school-lands being devoted to farms, truck-gardens, pastures, brick-yards, etc. Running through the grounds proper and extending the entire distance of the farms for two or three miles is a driveway, on either side of which, and on roads leading from it, are located the buildings of the Institute. These, for the most part, are brick structures, and have been built by the students

RESOURCES AND EQUIPMENT

themselves under the direction of their instructors in the various building trades. The plans for these buildings have been drawn in the architectural-drawing division of the Institute. While not as ornate as the buildings of some other institutions, they are substantial and well adapted to the uses for which they are intended. The newer buildings, constructed in the last ten years, are more artistic and imposing, showing great improvement in matters of architectural design and finish. Not only have the students performed the building operations that entered into the construction of these buildings, but they have also manufactured the brick, and have prepared much of the wooden and other materials that were used. We sometimes speak of a man as self-made, but I have never known another great educational institution that could be so described. Tuskegee, itself, is distinctively self-made.

Porter Hall was completed and occupied in the spring of 1883. The following year a brick building for girls was undertaken, and two years later completed. This building, named Alabama Hall, is rectangular in shape and four stories high. It contains a kitchen and dining-room, reception-rooms, apartments of the Dean of the Woman's

Department, and sleeping-rooms. There was no special gift made for this building, the money required for its erection being taken from the general funds of the Institute as they could be spared. A wing added later gave more space for dining-rooms and provided a number of sleeping-rooms.

The money used in putting up the buildings at Tuskegee is made to do double duty. In the first place, it provides the buildings for which it was primarily given, and, in the second place, furnishes opportunities for young men to learn the trades which are employed in their construction. Following closely upon the completion of Alabama Hall, there was begun another brick structure to be used as a dormitory for young men. Olivia Davidson Hall bears the honored name of the school's first and only Assistant Principal. Miss Davidson performed a conspicuous part in establishing the school and placing its claim for support before the public. This building is a four-story structure, and the first of the school's buildings for which the plans were made by the teacher of architectural drawing. The plans for all the buildings put up by the Institute are now made in the division of architectural drawing in charge of Mr. R. R. Tay-

RESOURCES AND EQUIPMENT

lor, a graduate of the Massachusetts Institute of Technology, who is ably assisted by Mr. W. S. Pittman, a graduate of Tuskegee and of the Drexel Institute in Philadelphia.

The need for a building to house the mechanical industries which, until 1892, had been conducted in temporary frame buildings on different parts of the grounds, led to the erection of Cassedy Hall, a three-story brick building standing at the east entrance to the grounds. Cassedy Hall, together with a smaller building devoted to a blacksmith shop and foundry, was used for the purpose mentioned, until three years ago, when all the industries for men were moved into the Slater-Armstrong Memorial Trades Building, at the opposite end of the grounds. Through the generosity of Mr. George F. Peabody, of New York, Cassedy 'Hall has since been converted into a dormitory for young men, and serves admirably for this purpose.

Phelps Hall, which is the Bible Training School Building, is the gift of two New York ladies who desired to do something to improve the Negro ministry. The building is of wood and has three stories, containing a lecture-hall, recitation-rooms, library, and sleeping-rooms for young men. A broad veranda extends entirely around the building.

TUSKEGEE AND ITS PEOPLE

Last year there were enrolled fifty-six students for the course in Bible Training, and among them were a number of ordained ministers who have regular charges. Phelps Hall was dedicated in 1892, Dr. Lyman Abbott preaching the dedicatory sermon and General Samuel C. Armstrong delivering an address, which was among his last public utterances.

In the next year Science Hall (now called Thrasher Hall, after the lamented Max Bennett Thrasher) was built. This is a handsome three-story building, with recitation-rooms and laboratories in the first two stories, and sleeping-rooms for teachers and boys in the third story. About this time a frame cottage with two stories and attic was built by the school as a residence for Mr. Washington. This he occupied until the gift of two Brooklyn friends enabled him to erect on his own lot, just opposite the school-grounds, his present handsome brick residence, where he dispenses a generous hospitality to the school's guests and to the teachers of the Institute. The cottage which he vacated was afterward utilized for a time as a library, but now is the home of Director Bruce of the Academic Department.

Alabama Hall, already mentioned, soon proved

RESOURCES AND EQUIPMENT

inadequate to meet the needs of the Woman's Department. A long one-story frame building, having the shape of a letter T, was then erected just in the rear of Alabama Hall. It has been used for girls' sleeping-rooms until this year, when it was taken down to make room for a park and playground for young women. There were also successively built for the growing demands of this department, and in the vicinity of the original girls' building, Willow Cottage, Hamilton Cottage, Parker Memorial Home, Huntington Hall, and only this last year Douglass Hall. Huntington Hall is the gift of Mrs. Collis P. Huntington. In design, finish, and appointments it is one of the best buildings owned by the school.

Three years ago a wealthy but unostentatious gentleman, who would not permit his name to be used in connection with his benefaction, gave the school $25,000 for a building for girls, suggesting that the structure should bear the name of some noted Negro. Douglass Hall was erected with this money and named in honor of that great leader of the race, Frederick Douglass. It is a two-story brick building, with a basement in its central section, and contains 40 sleeping-rooms, a reception-room, bathrooms, and a large assembly-room with a seating capacity of 450. In this room the Dean of the Woman's Department holds meetings with the girls on questions of health, morals, and manners. The building is heated with steam and lighted by electricity. All in all, Douglass Hall is the best of the buildings so far built by the Institute, and is a fitting monument to the man whose name it bears.

The Slater-Armstrong Memorial Agricultural Building was completed and dedicated in 1897. Hon. James Wilson, Secretary of Agriculture of the United States, honored the school by his presence and an address on the occasion of the formal opening of this building. It is a brick structure of two-and-a-half stories, with recitation-rooms, laboratory, museums, library, and an office for the use of the Department of Agriculture. In addition to its appropriation of $3,000 for the general work of the school, the State of Alabama makes an annual appropriation of $1,500 for the maintenance of an Agricultural Experiment Station. The plots of the Station and the school-farm are in close proximity to the Agricultural Building, and on these the young men taking the course in Agriculture put in practise the theories which they learn in the class-room. Many important experi-

RESOURCES AND EQUIPMENT

ments have been undertaken by the Station, of particular interest being those relating to soil building, the hybridization of sea-island cotton with some of the common short-staple varieties, fertilizer tests with potatoes, by which it has been shown that it is possible to raise as much as 266 bushels per acre on light, sandy soil such as that comprising the school-lands, while the average yield in the same part of Alabama is not more than 40 bushels to the acre.

The next building of importance to be put up after the Agricultural Building was the Chapel. Another gift from the two New York ladies who gave the money for Phelps Hall made possible this magnificent structure, admittedly one of the most imposing church edifices in the South. It is built of brick, 1,200,000 bricks entering into its construction, all of which were laid by student masons. It has stone trimmings, and in shape is a cross, the nave with choir having a length of 154 feet, and the distance through the transept being 106 feet. There are anterooms and a study for the Chaplain of the Institute. Including the gallery the seating capacity is 2,400. Here all gatherings of the school for religious and other purposes are now held. The great Tuskegee Negro Conference that

TUSKEGEE AND ITS PEOPLE

assembles in February of each year holds its meetings in the Chapel. Near the Chapel are the Barracks, two long, roughly constructed one-story frame buildings, which are used as sleeping quarters for young men until they can be better housed in permanent buildings.

Until 1900 the mechanical industries at Tuskegee were conducted in Cassedy Hall and some adjoining frame buildings. In that year they were moved into the commodious quarters which the then just completed Slater-Armstrong Memorial Trades Building furnished. This building is rectangular in shape, is built about a central court, and covers more space than any other of the school buildings. In its outside dimensions it is 283 feet by 315 feet. The front half of the building is two stories high, the rear half one story. It is constructed of brick, with a tin roof, and, like the other larger buildings at the Institute, has steam heat and electric light. The money for this building came in part from the J. W. and Belinda L. Randall Charities Fund of Boston and the steadfast friend of the school, Mr. George Foster Peabody, of New York. There is a tablet in the building bearing the following inscription: " This tablet is erected in memory of the generosity of

RESOURCES AND EQUIPMENT

J. W. and Belinda L. Randall, of Boston, Massachusetts, from whose estate $20,000 were received toward the erection of the building."

The various shops in this building are fairly well equipped with tools and apparatus to do the work required of them and to teach the trades pursued by the young men. Taking the Machine Division as an example, we find it supplied with one 18-inch lathe, one 14-inch lathe, one 20-inch planer, one 12-inch shaping-machine, one 20-inch drill-press, one $6\frac{1}{2}$-inch pipe-cutting and threading machine, one Brown and Sharpe tool-grinder, one sensitive drill-press, and, of course, the customary tools that go with these machines. The Electric-Lighting Plant is also located in this building. Not only does this Division light the buildings and grounds of the Institute, but it furnishes light to individuals in the town of Tuskegee, which is, at present, without other electric-lighting facilities.

In 1895 the school suffered the loss by fire of its well-appointed barn, together with some of its finest milch cows. This is the only serious fire that has occurred in the history of the school—a record almost unparalleled in an establishment so large. This fact has led to the school being able to get insurance at a lower rate than is generally given to educational institutions. It was not until 1900 that the school fully recovered from the loss of its barn. In this year friends in Brooklyn gave the money with which to rebuild the barn on a larger scale. It was deemed wise not to put all the money into one building, but to erect numbers of smaller ones and locate them so as to minimize the fire risk. Accordingly, plans were made to build a hennery, creamery, dairy-barn, horse-barn, carriage-house, tool-house, piggery, silos, and slaughter-house. All these buildings were at once put up, and are now giving effective service. At present the school owns 47 horses and colts, 76 mules, 495 cows and calves, 601 pigs, and 977 fowls of different kinds. These animals are all of good stock, some of them being thoroughbreds, and are cared for by the students who work in the Agricultural Department.

Dorothy Hall, the building which accommodates the Girls' Industrial Department, was built in 1901 on the side of the driveway opposite the Boys' Trades Building. This building is the gift of the two New York ladies who gave the Chapel and Phelps Hall. It serves its purpose admirably, the rooms being large, well lighted, and airy. Here are conducted all the trades taught to young women,

RESOURCES AND EQUIPMENT

including sewing, dressmaking, millinery, laundering, cooking, housekeeping, mattress-making, upholstering, broom-making, and basketry. As with the boys' trades, there is a very fair equipment of accessories for proper teaching.

In point of time, the next important building provided was the Carnegie Library, Mr. Carnegie giving $20,000 for the building and furnishings. The structure is two stories high, with massive Corinthian columns on the front. It contains, besides the library proper, a large assembly-room, an historical room, study-rooms, and offices for the Librarian. The building and the furniture are the product of student labor.

In 1901, with $2,000 given by Mrs. Quincy A. Shaw, of Boston, and $100 contributed by graduates of the Institute as a nucleus, the Children's House was built. This is a one-story frame building of good proportions, in which the primary school of the town is taught. It is the practise-school for students of the Institute who mean to teach. A kindergarten has also been established.

Mr. Rockefeller has given a dormitory for boys, which was completed and occupied last year. The lack of adequate sleeping quarters for young men, from which the school has suffered from the beginning, was very materially supplied in Rockefeller Hall, which is a three-story brick structure, furnishing accommodations for 150 students. This need for dormitories has been still further met through the gift of three brick cottages by Miss Julia Emery, an American now living in London. Two of these buildings were finished last year, and young men are now living in them. The third is nearing completion. All are two stories high, with a hall running through the middle, and contain 40 rooms of good size.

Until last year the offices of the Institute were scattered over the grounds wherever room could be found. A New York friend, who does not permit the use of his name, seeing the need of the school for a building in which the offices might be concentrated, thus greatly increasing the efficiency of its administrative work, gave $19,000 for this purpose. The Office Building, completed in the latter part of 1903, is the result of this benefaction. It is two-and-a-half stories high, and contains the offices of the Principal, the Principal's Secretary, Treasurer, Auditor, Business Agent, Commandant, Registrar, and the Post-Office and Savings Department.

THE OFFICE BUILDING IN PROCESS OF ERECTION.
Student carpenters shown at work.

RESOURCES AND EQUIPMENT

The most pretentious building owned by the Institute is the Collis P. Huntington Memorial Building, the new home of the Academic Department, which is the gift of Mrs. Huntington as a memorial to her husband, who was one of Tuskegee's stanchest supporters. It is built near the site of the original building, Porter Hall, which it displaces as the center of the academic work of the school. The outside dimensions are 183 feet by 103 feet. It is four stories in height. Besides recitation-rooms for all the classes, it contains a gymnasium in the basement for young women, and an assembly-room on the top floor capable of seating 800 persons. The finishing is in yellow pine. The buildings of the Institute show a steady progression in quality of workmanship, materials, and architectural design and efficiency, from the rather rough, wooden Porter Hall erected by hired workmen in 1882 to the stately Huntington Hall built by students in 1904.

Located at different points on the grounds and on lots detached are cottages occupied as residences by teachers and officers of the Institute.

The furnishings for all the buildings, as well as the buildings themselves, have been made by the students in the various shops, who at the same time were learning trades and creating articles of use.

The annual cost of conducting the institution is, in round numbers, $150,000. This may seem high, but when certain facts in regard to the work are borne in mind it will not appear exorbitant. In the first place, there are really three schools at Tuskegee—a day-school, a night-school, and a trade-school. Such a system makes necessary the employment of a larger number of teachers than would be needed in a purely academic institution holding only one session a day. Teachers in the trade-school, with special technical training, can be obtained only by paying them higher salaries than are paid to those who simply teach in the class-rooms.

Secondly, and principally, it is expensive to employ student labor to do the work of the school. By the time students become fairly proficient in their trades and reach the point where their services begin to be profitable, their time at the institution has expired, and a new, untrained set take their places, so that the school is constantly working on new material or raw recruits. Then, too, Tuskegee is still in the formative period of its growth as to buildings, laying-out and improve-

RESOURCES AND EQUIPMENT

ment of grounds, and equipment of its various departments. When the school's needs in these directions shall have been met, and the Negro parent shall become able to pay a larger share of the cost of educating his children, the expenses to the public of running the school may be materially reduced.

Money for the support of the school is derived principally from the following sources, viz.: The State of Alabama, $4,500; the John F. Slater Fund, $10,000; the General Education Board, $10,000; the Peabody Fund, $1,500; the Institute's Endowment Fund, $40,000; contributions of persons and charitable organizations, $84,000; a total of $150,000. The individual contributions are, for the most part, small, and come from persons of moderate means. Yet the institution annually receives some large gifts toward its expenses from those who are blessed with wealth.

Especial appeals are made by the institution for scholarships of $50 each, in order to pay the tuition of students who provide for their other expenses themselves largely by their work for the school, but who are unable to contribute anything toward the item of teaching. These scholarships are not turned over to the students, but are held

TUSKEGEE AND ITS PEOPLE

by the institution and assigned for their benefit, the aim being to do nothing for students which they can do for themselves, and thus help to develop in them a spirit of manly and womanly self-reliance.

The majority of the large donations, aside from those for endowment, have been for buildings and the purchase of additional farm-lands made necessary by the enlargement of the school's agricultural work.

What may be regarded as the greatest need of the institution is an adequate endowment which will put it upon a permanent basis and make its future certain.

A gratifying beginning in the building up of an endowment has already been made. It is a fact, still well remembered by the public, that Mr. Andrew Carnegie has given to the endowment fund the princely sum of $600,000. Before that time $400,000 had been collected from other sources for the same purpose, the largest single contribution toward this amount being $50,000 from the late Collis P. Huntington.

As already stated, the income from the present endowment is $40,000, out of which several annuities are paid. This is only a little more than one-

RESOURCES AND EQUIPMENT

fourth of the amount that must be had each year to pay the expenses of the school. It will require an endowment of at least $3,000,000 to yield an income adequate to the present needs of the institution alone.

III

THE ACADEMIC AIMS

By Roscoe Conkling Bruce

THE Negro needs industrial training in eminent degree, because the capacity for continuous labor is a requisite of civilized living; because, indeed, the very first step in social advance must be economic; because the industrial monopoly with which slavery encompassed black men has fallen shattered before the trumpet-blast of white labor and eager competition; and, finally, because no instrument of moral education is more effective upon the mass of mankind than cheerful and intelligent work. These ideas powerfully voiced, together with an unusually magnanimous attitude toward the white South, have set the man who toiled doggedly up from slavery, upon a hill apart. These things are distinctive of this man; they suggest his temper, his spirit, his point of view; but they do not exhaust his interests. Similarly, the distinctive feature of Tuskegee—adequate provision for industrial training—sets it upon a hill apart, but

ROSCOE C. BRUCE.
Director of the Academic Department.

THE ACADEMIC AIMS

by a whimsical perversity this major feature is in some quarters assumed to be the whole school. A moment's reflection shows such a view to be mistaken.

The very industries at Tuskegee presuppose a considerable range of academic study. Tuskegee does not graduate hoe-hands or plowboys. Agriculture is, of course, fundamental—fundamental in recognition of the fact that the Negro population is mainly a farming population, and of the truth that something must be done to stem the swelling tide which each year sweeps thousands of black men and women and children from the sunlit monotony of the plantation to the sunless iniquity of the slums, from a drudgery that is not quite cheerless to a competition that is altogether merciless. But the teaching of agriculture, even in its elementary stages, presupposes a considerable amount of academic preparation. To be sure, a flourishing garden may be made and managed by bright-eyed tots just out of the kindergarten, but how can commercial fertilizers be carefully analyzed by a boy who has made no study of general chemistry? and how can a balanced ration be adjusted by an illiterate person? Similarly, the girl in the laundry does not make soap by rote, but by principle; and the girl in the dressmaking-shop does not cut out her pattern by luck, or guess, or instinct, or rule of thumb, but by geometry. And so the successful teaching of the industries demands no mean amount of academic preparation. In this lies the technical utility of Tuskegee's Academic Department.

Then, too, a public service has been rendered by Hampton and Tuskegee in showing that industrial training—the system in which the student learns by doing and is paid for the commodities he produces—may be so managed as to educate. Among the excellencies of industrial training, I would state that the severe commercial test in which sentiment plays no part is applied as consistently to the student's labor as is the force of gravitation to a falling body. Here we must keep in mind the unavoidably concrete nature of the product, whether satisfactory or not; the discipline such training affords in organized endeavor; the stimulus it offers to all the virtues of a drudgery which, though it repel an unusually ardent and sensitive temperament, yet wears a precious jewel in its head; and an exceptionally keen sense of responsibility, since on occasion large amounts of money and the esteem of the school at large and

THE ACADEMIC AIMS

the lives of a student's fellows depend upon his circumspection and skill. Such training educates.

But that would indeed be a sorry program of education which blinked the fact that the student must be rendered responsive to the nobler ideals of the human race, that his eyes must be opened to the immanent values of life. If a clear title to forty acres and a mule represents the extreme upper limit of a black man's ambition, why call him a man? If a bank-account represents the sum of his happiness, that happiness lacks humanity. If you would educate for life, you must arouse spiritual interests. "The life is more than meat, and the body than raiment." Through history and literature the Tuskegee student is brought to develop a criticism, an appreciation of life and the worthier ends of human striving. To such a discipline, however elementary, the critic will not, I take it, begrudge the name "education."

And if the reader wavers in contemplating the problems of trudging Negroes, remember that the type of Negro who is a menace to the community is he who, in moments of leisure, responds to somewhat grosser incentives than the poetry of Longfellow, the romance of Hawthorne, and the philosophy of Emerson. I would reassure your idealism with this counsel of prudence.

Another question presses: Does the value of Tuskegee lie in the fact that the school equips for happy lives merely as many persons as are subjected to the immediate play of its influences; that its circle of efficiency includes only as many as are enrolled in its various courses? To that question every teacher in the school and the mass of graduates and students would give an emphatic, a decisive, No! The real value of the school lies in the service rendered to the people of the communities where our young folks go to live and labor. Now, work in wood and iron, however assiduously prosecuted, never erected in any human being's heart a passion for social service; a finer material must be used, a material finer than gold. And so the plan and deeper intent of Tuskegee Institute are incapable of realization without the incentives supplied by history and literature.

Finally, there is a trade for which the academic studies, supplemented by specific normal instruction, are the direct preparation—teaching school. In the census year there were over 21,000 Negro school-teachers in the United States, and in the decade 1890–1900 the ratio of increase was more

THE ACADEMIC AIMS

than twice as rapid as that of the Negro population; but, nevertheless, there were in 1900 more than twice as many teachers in the South per 10,000 white children as per 10,000 colored. But such data can not even approximately indicate the relative amounts of teaching enjoyed by these two classes of children, for the statistical method can not express the incalculable disparity in teaching-efficiency.

A friend of mine—a graduate of Brown University—was for several years a member of a board which corrected the examination-papers of Negro candidates for teachers' certificates in a certain Southern State where the school facilities for the Negro population are exceptionally good; but he confessed to me that repeatedly not a paper submitted deserved a passing mark, but the board was "simply compelled to grant certificates in order to provide teachers enough to go around." Nor is such a dearth of black pedagogues in the least extraordinary. The mission of Tuskegee Institute is largely to supply measurably well-equipped teachers for the schools—teachers able and eager to teach gardening and carpentry as well as grammar and arithmetic, teachers who seek to organize the social life of their communities upon wholesome principles, tactfully restraining grossness and unobtrusively proffering new and nobler sources of enjoyment. And so the academic studies are wrought into the essential scheme of Tuskegee's work.

Let us inspect with some closeness the organization of the institution. The student-body is fundamentally divided into day-students and night-students. The night-students work in the industries, largely at common labor, all day and every day, and go to school at night, thus paying their current board bills, and accumulating such credits at the Treasurer's office as will later defray their expenses in the day-school. The day-school students are divided perpendicularly through the classes into two sections, section No. 1 working in the industries every other day for three days a week and attending academic classes the remaining three days, while this situation is exactly reversed for section No. 2. Thus every week-day half of each day-school class is in the Academic Department, while the other half is in the Industrial. This arrangement induces a wholesome rivalry between the students of the two sections, and effects an equal distribution of the working force and skill over every week-day.

THE ACADEMIC AIMS

The day-school students consist, then, of two classes of persons: those who, as night-students, have accumulated credits sufficient to pay their way in the day-school, and those whose families are able to pay a considerable part of their expenses. The earnings of a student in the day-school can not be large enough to pay his current board bill, but such a student is ordinarily enjoying the valuable advantage of working at one of the more skilled trades.

The night-school student, perhaps, because of greater maturity in years and experience, may be relied upon to apply himself with the utmost diligence to his academic studies; so, in much less than half the time-allotment, he advances in his academic studies about half as fast as the day-school student. This schedule did not spring full-fledged from the seething brain of any theorist; it is no fatuous imitation of the educational practise of some remote and presumptively dissimilar institution; it has, so to say, elaborated itself in adjustment to the actual needs of the particular situation. This provision boasts not of novelty, but of utility; though not ideal, it is practicable. But the central fact is that this Tuskegee Plan, while clearly securing ample time for the teaching of the industries, makes possible no mean amount of academic study.

In order more clearly to exhibit the grounds of this proposition, I shall refer in some slight detail to the course of study in English and in Mathematics.

Mathematics represents the group of academic studies which possess direct technical value for the industries; moreover, it is a pretty good index of the grades comprehended in the Academic Department. In the lowest class in the day-school—there is one lower in the night-school—the arithmetical tables are mastered, and fractions introduced and developed with the use of liquid, dry, surface, and time measures; whereas in the Senior class algebra is studied through quadratics and plane geometry through the "area of polygons." That is to say, the lowest day-school class is about equivalent to a fourth grade in the North, and the Senior to the first or the second year (barring the foreign languages) in a Northern high school.

Despite a much smaller time-allotment, our students, roughly speaking, keep pace with Northern students because they are older and somewhat more serious, because the course is shortened by the elimination of uselessly perplexing topics in arith-

A PORTION OF THE SCHOOL GROUNDS.

THE ACADEMIC AIMS

metic like compound proportion and cube root, but chiefly because the utility of mathematics is made vivid, and vigorous interest aroused by its immediate application in class-room and shop to problems arising in the industries. Our students are not stuffed like sausages with rules and definitions, mathematical or other; they ascend to general principles through the analysis of concrete cases.

English serves to represent the group of studies that exert a liberalizing influence upon the student, that possess a cultural rather than a technical value. From oral lessons in language in the lower classes, the students advance to a modicum of technical grammar in the middle of the course, and hence to the rhetoric of the Senior year. Moreover, an unusually large amount of written composition is insisted upon, the compositions being used not merely to discipline the student in chaste feeling, consecutive thinking, and efficient expression, but also to sharpen his powers of observation and to stimulate him to pick out of his daily experience the elements that are significant. School readers are used in the lower classes because the readers present economically and compactly a whole gamut of literary styles and forms. These readers are importantly supplemented and gradually superseded by certain classics appropriate to the grades. The classic, whether Robinson Crusoe, or Ivanhoe, Rip Van Winkle, the House of Seven Gables, or The Merchant of Venice, presents an artistic whole, and permits the students to acquire some sense of literary structure. The dominant motive in literary instruction is, perhaps, esthetic, but I am convinced that the ethical influence of this instruction at Tuskegee is profound and abiding.

However liberal the provisions of the academic curriculum, the value of the department is finally determined by the devotion and ability of the teachers. Universities and normal schools, and the seasoned staffs of public-school systems—from these sources, whether in Massachusetts, California, or Tennessee, Principal Washington has gathered a force of academic teachers of rare ability and devotion. Eminent for personality rather than for method, these teachers are no tyros in method. In such hands the excellent features of the curriculum are raised to the N-th power.

Finally, academic and industrial teachers are animated with a sentiment of solidarity, with an esprit de corps, which solves many a problem of conflicting duty and jurisdiction, and which must impress the student with the essential unity of Tus-

ANOTHER PORTION OF THE SCHOOL GROUNDS.

THE ACADEMIC AIMS

kegee's endeavor to equip men and women for life. The crude, stumbling, sightless plantation-boy who lives in the environment of Tuskegee for three or four years, departs with an address, an alertness, a resourcefulness, and above all a spirit of service, that announce the educated man.

IV

WHAT GIRLS ARE TAUGHT, AND HOW

By Mrs. Booker T. Washington

"We wants our baby gal, Mary Lou, to come up to Tuskegee to git eddicated and learn seamstress; kase we doesn't want her to work lak we is," says the farmer. "I wish to help you plant this new industry, broom-making," writes Miss Susan B. Anthony, "because you are trying so earnestly to teach your girls other means of livelihood besides sewing, housework, and cooking." This is the problem we have been trying to solve at Tuskegee for over twenty years: What handiwork can we give our girls with their academic training that will better fit them to meet the demand for skilled teachers in the various avenues of the industrial and academic world now opening so rapidly to women?

Learning to sew, with the ultimate end of becoming a full-fledged dressmaker, has been the

MRS. BOOKER T. WASHINGTON.
Director of Industries for Girls.

WHAT GIRLS ARE TAUGHT

height of ambition with the major part of our girls when brought to the institution by their horny-handed fathers and mothers fresh from the soil of Alabama, Georgia, Tennessee, or Florida. After the last gripless hand-shake, with the tremulous, " Take care of yourself, honey," the hard-working father and mother have turned their faces homeward, visibly affected by the separation, but resolved to shoulder the sacrifice of the daughter's much-needed help on the plantation, which oftentimes is all that they are able to contribute toward her education.

Not infrequently the girl has begun in the lowest class in night-school. Her parents send her articles of clothing now and then on Christmas; but the largest contributions to her wardrobe come from the boxes and barrels sent to the institution by Northern friends. She has remained in school during the summer vacation, and within two years has entered day-school with enough to her credit to finish her education. When the happy parents return to see their daughter graduated, after six or seven long years, their faces are radiant because of their realized hopes. When they see their white-robed daughter transformed from the girl they brought here clad in the homespun of the old days, and receiving her certificate, the tears come unchecked, and the moving lips no doubt form a whispered prayer.

In a recent class there was graduated a young woman of twenty-five. She came to the school in her eighteenth year from the " piney woods " of Alabama. She entered the lowest preparatory class in night-school and was assigned to work in the laundry. She was earnest and faithful in work and study. She passed on from class to class, remaining at school to work during the vacation. After two years in the laundry she was given an opportunity to learn plain sewing in that division. She was promoted to the Dressmaking Division at the end of the year, and received her certificate at the close of two years, after working every day and attending night-school. She spent the last two years of her school life in the Millinery Division, and received her certificate from that division with one from the Academic Department on her graduation. During these two years she taught the sewing-classes in the night-school of the town of Tuskegee. At the outset she bought the materials used with $1, left over from the sales of the previous year. From this small nest-egg as a starter, seventeen girls were supplied with work. But so

WHAT GIRLS ARE TAUGHT

efficient and frugal was the young teacher that she sold articles, bought supplies for her class, and ended the year with $3.45 in the treasury.

This is just a leaf from the history of one girl. Of the 520 girls entering the institution during this year (1903–'04), 458 have remained for the full scholastic year. About 50 per cent came from country districts all over the United States. A large majority of them asked to enter the Dressmaking Division to learn that trade; but after the field of industries was opened to their view, they were scattered about in the different divisions, a very large per cent still leaning to the side of dressmaking and millinery.

Taking into account the number of girls working their way through at their trades by day and attending night-school, they were distributed as follows: Horticulture, 4; training-kitchen, 13; housekeeping, 38; dining-room, 29; hospital, 20; kitchen-gardening, 8; poultry-raising, 7; tailoring, 14; dairying, 10; printing, 6; broom-making, 26; mattress-making, 18; upholstering, 18; laundering, 54; plain sewing, 72; millinery, 51; dressmaking, 69. All the girls were required to take cooking twice a week and 209 of the girls in the normal classes took basketry.

TUSKEGEE AND ITS PEOPLE

As the trades were the great attraction in the school curriculum, it was deemed necessary to separate the school into two divisions, that students might have an opportunity to receive instruction equally in the Academic and Industrial Departments. This year this scheme worked successfully by an arrangement that placed one division in the Academic Department on Mondays, Wednesdays, and Fridays, while the other was at work, and the other division in the Trades Department on Thursdays, Fridays, and Saturdays, while the other was in school, and so on regularly.

Girl life at Tuskegee is strenuous. Though study and work are constantly to the fore, character is effectively developed with brain and muscle, and the well-earned recreation-hour comes just frequently enough to lend the highest source of pleasure. Though the girl usually comes with a hazy conception of what the days in school will really mean for the ripening of those powers that she earnestly intends to use for the best development of herself, there is always a spirit of learning, that she may be of service to others. That is what counts in the school-days of the average girl in her struggle for more light.

The girl, coming a stranger from her home

WHAT GIRLS ARE TAUGHT

in the city or country, is lost in a crowd of girls new to dormitory life. New surroundings and new conditions are everywhere. New emotions, new purposes, new resolutions chase one another in her thoughts, and she becomes a stranger to herself only to find her bearings first in her own room. Here Maine and California, far-away Washington and Central America, meet on common ground. Alabama and Georgia alone feel kinship from geographical propinquity.

Beds, one double and one single, chairs, a table, mirror, bookcase, wardrobe, wash-stand, and screen, all manufactured on the grounds, compose the simple furniture of the room. But a few pictures, a strip of carpet before each bed, a bright table-covering, soon give the room the appearance of home, and the untried life has begun. The duty-list assigns to each girl her work, and perhaps the first lessons in order and system will be fairly instituted.

How many and varied are the associations that cluster about the life of the girl in her room, that refuge from a day of discouragement in schoolroom or workshop, and a haven of peace during the quiet hours of the Sabbath! Roommate meets roommate, quick to resent and as quick to forgive—

and the petty strife and envy suppressed at birth only serve to discipline them for the coming days.

Up with the rising bell at five, the duties of the room are almost finished when the girl leaves her beds to air while she takes her six o'clock breakfast. Social amenities, the niceties of table-training, and the tricks of speech that betray the sectional birthright, proclaim to the ever-observant table-mates the status of each newcomer, and she rises or falls in estimation just so far as her metal rings true. Thus another element enters into her life, one that will prove a potent force in balancing character; for the frankly expressed criticisms of schoolmates play no small part in the development of students.

If a girl be one of the forty-five waitresses on the eighty-nine tables of the dining-room, she eats her breakfast as the other students march out, then finishes her room-duties and is ready for work at ten minutes of seven wherever she happens to be assigned. If she is a dishwasher, she does that work, waits for inspection of the table that she has set, finishes her room-duty, and is admitted into her work division at half past seven.

Gardening and greenhouse work are becoming so attractive through the Nature-Study classes of the Academic Department that there are constant

WHAT GIRLS ARE TAUGHT

applications for transfers from the sewing divisions to this outside work. Equipped in an overall gingham apron and sunbonnet of the same material, the girl begins her duties, and no prouder girl can be found than she who takes her first basket of early spring vegetables to the Teachers' Home.

If the day is to be spent with the whole agricultural force of girls picking strawberries for the tables of the Boarding Department and the local market, the stage takes the group out to the patch two miles back on the farm—and that is happiness unalloyed for the schoolgirl. When she correlates her outing with her school work on the day following, there is seen nature at first-hand in the classroom.

If other classmates have been working in the Plain-Sewing Division turning out cotton underwear and plain articles of clothing to supply the demand of the Salesroom of the institution, the lesson in English has a natural, practical bearing, arising from the fact that one hour has been spent with the theory class of the workroom studying the warp and woof of the materials used, perhaps the sixth or seventh lesson in a series on cotton, introduced to the class first in its native heath. Correlation comes in wherever it may, and the association of ideas obtained in class-room and workroom is closely joined.

The large class of the Dressmaking Division, spending the day from seven until half past five making the blue uniform dresses, filling orders for tailor-made dresses in silk and cloth, measuring, drafting, cutting, and fitting, has many a representative in the schoolroom the succeeding day; and still more is the lesson varied by the practical illustrations in Mathematics or the recital of the experiences of the day in the English classes.

The girl in the millinery work, shaping forms, trimming hats, blending colors, drawing designs, studying textiles and fabrics for analysis in her theory classes twice during her three days of work, finds added inspiration for her three days of classroom study. If she is in the Senior class, she specializes in geometry on her school-days and mechanical drawing on her work-days. When our girl has finished her course in drawing and begins one of the uniform hats worn by the hundreds of girls, she ranks among the first milliners of the land in the estimation of the beginners. She completes hat after hat, drapes them until the number meets the requirement, and then comes her own

A CLASS IN MILLINERY.

WHAT GIRLS ARE TAUGHT

creation, a pattern hat, undersized of course, but a real dress hat and a thing of beauty. It usually finds its way to the old home for her mother and neighbors to admire. The commendation that comes back to the school is worth its weight in gold.

But there are backward learners. Some there are who excel in embroidery, crocheting, making ties and other fancy articles, but who have no aptitude for shaping and trimming hats. They plod on, and win at last. Then there is the girl whose parents wish her to open a millinery establishment in their town. She tries, but finally agrees with her long-suffering instructor that she would succeed at mattress-making and upholstering instead.

The work in the Mattress Division begins with sheet, pillow-case, table-linen, and comforter-making for the endless demands of the lodging division of the boys and girls. Pulling shucks for the mattress is the next step in advance, and when shucks are covered by the cotton layers in the making, they prove an excellent substitute for the hair filling of a more expensive manufacture, and they have an advantage in the matter of cleanliness. Covering screen frames made in the Carpentry Division for the numerous rooms, caning couches, rockers, and stools, help add to the variety of work in the division. The girl is not awarded her certificate until she has completed the round of work, including the fashioning of a bedroom suite from barrels finally covered with neat-figured denim. The semiweekly theory classes are not unlike those of the plain-sewing division, and the girl is as proud of her achievement with needle, hammer, and saw as if she were an adept in lighter work.

When the machinery was introduced for Broom-making, the girls looked askance at the appliances. But when the broom-corn was delivered from the farm, and the pioneer girl broom-maker began threshing off the seed in the cleaner, an interest was evinced that has increased with the knowledge that the work, study, or manufacture (call it what you will) is very productive, especially in the confines of the girls' broom-factory at Tuskegee Institute. The poultry-yard bought the seeds threshed off the broom-stalks; the hundreds of old handles collected cost nothing, and when the wiring, stitching, and clipping were finished and the girl saw the first broom turned out, there was triumph in the fact that the industry was the most inexpensive and still the most productive of credit of all the girls' industries under the roof of Dorothy Hall. The evolution from the flag-straw

WHAT GIRLS ARE TAUGHT

broom used in cabins of the South to the ones now completed and labeled, creates the sensation of the girl-world in the trades school. The wonders brought out in the theory class in connection with broom-making were marvelous. Broom-making has come to remain with our other girls' industries.

Work in the Laundry presents another aspect to the onlooker, and he doubtless decides on the spur of the moment that all is drudgery here. Girls are then assorting countless pieces received on Mondays from students and teachers. They are placing the assorted articles in cages in the basement. Two boys are filling three washers with bed-linen, and in another apartment two girls are weighing and measuring materials to make more soap to add to the boxes standing in the soap-room. Girls up-stairs in the wash-room are busy rubbing at the tubs. Some girls are starching, and others are sending baskets down on the elevator for girls below to hang in the drying-room. Others are in the assorting-room putting away clothes-bags into numerous boxes. The ironing-room farther on is filled with busy workers. Days come during every week when time is spent in the study of laundry chemistry. Rust and mildew stains and scorching are some of the problems of the Laundry, and they find solution. Soap, starch, water, and bluing have their composite qualities and are analyzed, and no more interesting correlation is there than that of the laundry with the class-room.

Although each Tuskegee girl is expected to become proficient in one trade at least, all are required to attend the cooking classes. Girls belonging to certain classes are scattered in the various divisions, each busily engaged at her chosen trade. At the ringing of the bells in each division at stated hours, classes form and pass to the training-kitchen for their lesson in cooking. Both night-school and day-school girls report every day until every girl has received her lesson weekly. The normal classes have theory and practise one hour each, the preparatory girls one hour weekly for their trades.

This is true also of girls in the normal classes. They spend one hour in basketry study, making in all three hours away from their individual trades each week. Theory is combined with practise, and many a fanciful thought is woven in with the reed and raffia of the Indian baskets, African purses, belts, and pine-needle work-baskets. The shuck hats and foot-mats are so foreign in design that one often wonders how it were possible to utilize

WHAT GIRLS ARE TAUGHT

the same material in so widely different purposes. But our girl is progressive, and not a few instances have occurred when one has been informed of the presence of a Tuskegee student in a remote country district, by the inevitable shuck hat prettily designed and worn by an utter stranger. So remunerative has been the work that many have earned money enough from the sales of these hats to purchase books for the school year and pay their entrance fees.

Few girls work at typesetting. Those learning the trade are in the Boys' Trades Building. The same is true of the girl tailors, who are as capable workers in the trade as the boys. The majority of these girls are in night-school, and of late years have not earned much for their work. In former years the greater body of the students were working their way through school, and by their labor would earn enough to complete their education in the Academic Department and the Industrial as well. Last year the pay schedule was reduced, and many appeals for assistance came from those battling their way through. A young girl whose monthly statement warned her that she owed the school $15, at the end of the school year wrote the following:

TUSKEGEE AND ITS PEOPLE

"DEAR MRS. WASHINGTON: I write to inform you of the enormous sum that I owe on my board bill. I am not satisfied, because I want to earn something in life, but it seems that means and opportunity will not permit me. I can't help from crying when I think how anxious and willing my people are to help me to be something, and yet they are unable to help me.

"My mother has struggled to bring up eight of us, and now is to the point where she can give me no more help, and that leaves me alone to be something by myself. I am anxious to enter day-school so I may finish my course of study and my trade, and at last let my mother see me a good, noble woman, who will take care of her.

"I will thank you very much for your kindness, if you will look into my board bill and help me as soon, and as much, as possible. Yours gratefully."

As the day girls have put in so many hours of work recently under the new system, it eliminates the necessity of so many night-school girls being paid for their work. It is to the interest of the school and its day-students that fewer work their way through school, and the time has come to teach this fact. The boy or girl for a time will stagger in the attempt to gain education, but will be all the more able, later, to reach the desired goal.

WHAT GIRLS ARE TAUGHT

All girls are taught housekeeping incidentally in the care of their rooms; but the number assigned to the regular division yearly are instructed in all branches of home industry. The course covering two years is mapped out thoroughly, and when the girls reach the Senior class, all have their turn at housekeeping in the Practise Cottage of four rooms. No girl is graduated from the school without the finishing touch of the little home. Marketing, the planning of meals, table-setting, the care of table- and bed-linen, dusting, sweeping, and everything else pertaining to a well-kept house, are taught by the teacher in domestic science who is in charge of the training-kitchen where the senior girls received their first lessons in cookery. The young housekeepers have reached the stage of efficiency when they may prepare a meal for a distinguished guest.

A red-letter day in the history of the cottage came when a warm-hearted and much-beloved trustee of the institution expressed a wish to dine with the girls during one of his visits to the institution. The flowers that graced the small table on this day were brought by the distinguished visitor, who came from a stroll in the "piney" woods. The girls, apprehensive of their success in preparing the dinner for one with so cultured a palate, felt visibly relieved on the disappearance of the roast, the vegetables, and the dessert. The corn bread was voted the best ever eaten, and the dinner, as a whole, a delicious preparation. If ever, in the years to come, any of the four forgets the kindly heart that made all forget station or condition, "the right hand will forget its cunning."

Days pass all too quickly in work and study. After the supper at six, the girls in the normal classes go to their rooms or the Carnegie Library for study, the girls in the preparatory classes go to the study-hour, and those who have been working at the trades during the day spend two hours in night-school covering half as much ground as those in day-school, and consequently spend a longer period in school. At the ringing of the bell at half past eight all the girls form in line to pass to the Chapel for prayers.

School and work over for the day, every girl seems to lose her personality in her blue braided uniform, with her red tie and turnover on weekday evenings at Chapel, and her white ribbon on Sundays when she passes the platform as she marches by out of the Chapel to her room. Her carriage at least identifies her class-standing, and

WHAT GIRLS ARE TAUGHT

one may easily note the difference in the manner of her who has newly arrived and another who has been in school with the advantages of several years.

Friday afternoons mark an hour for lectures, girls' clubs, and circle entertainments. Saturday evenings are spent optionally. Time for class gymnastics or sewing or swimming is always spent pleasantly on schedule time during the week. Our girl attends the Christian Endeavor Sunday mornings at nine, Chapel at eleven, Sunday-school at one, and, after dinner is out of the way, spends the enforced quiet hour in her room from three until four o'clock reading. The band concert on the lawn calls all to listen, some walking, some sitting on the seats on the green, but all presenting a picturesque appearance in the blue skirts and white waists of the spring season.

Thus the days and weeks pass, mingled with the sorrows and joys of school-life, its encouragements and disappointments. The months and seasons come and go, and, before one is scarcely aware of the fact, the Commencement Week is here and the hundreds of young people whose lives have come in touch with one another pass on to their homes. Some go out as helpful workers, giving

TUSKEGEE AND ITS PEOPLE

useful service to others; many will return to complete the course begun, but all, we hope, will give out the light that will not fail. Some are workers with ten talents, some with five, some with one; but all, we trust, will be using them for the upbuilding of the kingdom here on earth.

V

HAMPTON INSTITUTE'S RELATION TO TUSKEGEE

BY ROBERT R. MOTON

IN his eloquent address in May, 1903, at the memorial services of General Samuel Chapman Armstrong, Founder, and for twenty-five years Principal, of Hampton Institute, Dr. Booker T. Washington said: "A few nights ago, while I was driving through the woods in Alabama, I discerned in the distance a large, bright fire. Driving to it, I soon found out that by the glow of this fire several busy hands were building a nice frame cottage, to replace a log cabin that had been the abode of the family for a quarter of a century. That fire was lighted by General Armstrong years ago. What does it matter that it was twenty-five years passing through Hampton to Tuskegee and through the Tuskegee Conference to that lonely spot in those lonely woods! It was doing its work very effectually all the same, and will continue to do it through the years to come."

The relations existing between Tuskegee Institute and Hampton Institute are much like those existing between a son and the father who has watched the growth and development of his child through the formative transition periods of his youth, and looks with pride upon him as he stands forth in the full bloom of manhood, enumerating successes already achieved, with large promise of greater and more far-reaching achievements for the immediate future. The child never reaches the point where he does not seek the approval and blessing of the parent, or where he refuses to accept advice and assistance if needed.

In the early days of Tuskegee Mr. Washington turned naturally and properly to Hampton for anything that was needed, as he so beautifully and repeatedly testifies in his autobiography, Up from Slavery. For a long time the men and women who helped him were from Hampton, more than fifty such having been there.

While there is a large number of Hampton graduates in the Industrial Departments of Tuskegee, the teaching force, especially in the Academic Department, represents a dozen or more of the best colleges and universities in this country. The same may be said of Hampton.

Up to about eight or ten years ago we at

HAMPTON INSTITUTE

Hampton spoke of Tuskegee as a small Hampton, but "small" no longer describes Tuskegee, and I doubt seriously if *large Hampton* would be altogether proper.

While Tuskegee was founded on the Hampton plan, and has consistently followed that plan as far as possible, and while these two great "Industrial Universities" are very much alike in spirit and purpose, they are, on the other hand, very dissimilar in external appearance as well as in internal conduct. Each sends out into the benighted districts of the South, and Hampton also into the Indian country of the West, hundreds of men and women who are living influences of civilization and Christianity in their deepest and most far-reaching sense, adding much to the solution of the perplexing questions with which the nation has to deal.

The conditions surrounding the two schools have necessitated certain differences in their evolution. The personnel of the two institutions is different. Hampton has always been governed and controlled by white people, and its teachers have come from the best families of the North. Tuskegee was founded by a Negro, and its teachers and officers have come from the best types of the American Negro and from the best schools opened to them. Hampton deals with a different class of student material, including the Indian, who is almost as different in traits and characteristics from the Negro as he is in feature and origin. These are, in a sense, external differences which must of necessity affect the character and internal machinery of the two institutions.

This is no reflection upon either school, for each is unique and complete in its way, and any marked ethnic change in the management of either would be unfortunate. Hampton is a magnificent illustration of Anglo-Saxon ideas in modern education. Tuskegee, on the other hand, is the best demonstration of Negro achievement along distinctly altruistic lines. In its successful work for the elevation and civilization of the children of the freedmen, it is also the most convincing evidence of the Negroes' ability to work together with mutual regard and mutual helpfulness. When Tuskegee was started there was a serious question as to whether Negroes could in any large measure combine for business or educational purposes. The only cooperative institutions that had been successful among them were the Church and, perhaps, the secret societies.

HAMPTON INSTITUTE

In material development, in the rapid and steadily improving accession of student material, in enlarging powers for greater usefulness, in influence upon the educational methods of the country and the civilized world, and in the sympathy and respect it has gained for the Negro through the writings and speeches of its Founder and Principal, the Tuskegee Institute has without doubt passed beyond the expectations of those who were most sanguine about its future.

The Tuskegee torch, from the Hampton fire started so many years ago by General Armstrong, has spread and is spreading light to thousands of homes and communities throughout the South, and is the greatest pride and glory of Hampton Institute, and a constant source of inspiration and encouragement to the devoted men and women who have always made Hampton's work possible.

At the conclusion of an address in a Northern city in the interest of Hampton, in which I had quoted Dr. Curry's saying that, "if Hampton had done nothing more than to give us Booker Washington, its history would be immortality," a New England lady of apparently good circumstances and well informed, in the kindness of her heart, took me to task for distorting my facts in saying

TUSKEGEE AND ITS PEOPLE

that Tuskegee had grown out of Hampton. She was sure that it was just the other way—that Hampton was an offshoot of Tuskegee. She certainly could not have paid a higher tribute to Hampton, and likewise to Tuskegee.

For the past few years Mr. Washington's deserved popularity and prominence have brought Tuskegee conspicuously and constantly before the public. This has in no sense been a disadvantage to Hampton, but has been a distinct gain in enabling Hampton to point to the foremost man of the Negro race, and to the largest and most interesting and in many ways the best-managed institution of the race, as the best and most conspicuous product of the peculiar kind of education for which Hampton stands.

While Tuskegee is, perhaps, in many respects, better known than Hampton, its antecedent, Hampton, is without doubt much better known and more highly thought of because of the existence of Tuskegee.

Tuskegee in its present state of development would be one of the marvels of the age, even if the personality of its Principal were left out of consideration.

Two thousand Negroes who are scarcely a

HAMPTON INSTITUTE

generation removed from bondage, being trained, disciplined, controlled by 200 or more of the same racial type; 2,000 Negroes being educated, morally, industrially, intellectually; an industrial university with 100 large buildings well equipped and beautifully laid-off grounds, with a hum and bustle of industry, scientifically and practically conducted by a race considered as representing the lowest ethnic type, upsetting the theories of many well-meaning people who believe the Negroes incapable of maintaining themselves in this civilization, incapable of uniting in any successful endeavor without being under the direct personal control of the dominant Aryan—this is one of the greatest achievements of the race during its years of freedom.

Hampton, though a dozen years older, the pioneer in industrial education, equally well equipped, quite as well conducted, doing as great a work in the elevation of the races it represents, and holding just as important a place in the scheme of modern education, is not so interesting or so wonderful, because its conception and execution are the product of Aryan thought and Aryan ingenuity. New ideas, new discoveries, new inventions and organizations, new methods and new institutions, have been conspicuous among the white race for a thousand years. General Armstrong's wisdom and foresight were truly wonderful, as indeed are also those of his worthy successor, Dr. H. B. Frissell, under whose direction the school's influence and usefulness have steadily increased, and along lines that General Armstrong would approve; but had Hampton been founded and brought to its present state of proficiency by a Negro, and its dominating force been of the African race, it would be a more wonderful and interesting institution. In other words; the white race has long since passed its experimental period. It now is the standard of measurement for all other races. The Negro's achievements, then, are considered largely with reference to the impression which they make upon the race of whose civilization and government he is a part.

Tuskegee, therefore, stands out more prominently than Hampton as an exponent of industrial education, and has been more severely questioned because of the imagined disloyalty in a Negro's aggressive attitude for this particular kind of education for his race. There are people of both races who, while they do not on the whole oppose Hampton and Tuskegee in their educational methods, are honestly afraid that, because of the growing

THE EXECUTIVE COUNCIL.

HAMPTON INSTITUTE

importance and influence of these two schools and others of a similar kind, the idea will be thoroughly established that the Negro needs only and is capable only of the narrowest sort of industrial training—such as is represented by the "rule-of-thumb carpenter" and the "one-suspender mule-driver," who work by rule and rote rather than by principle and method, not in the slightest degree comprehending the science underlying the work in which they are engaged, whose mathematical knowledge is bounded by "the distance between two corn or cotton rows."

To fix such an idea in the minds of the people of this country—which is not likely to be done—would, no doubt, be disastrous to us for generations to come, and make it much more easy than it is now to deprive the Negro of the civil and political rights which are guaranteed by the Constitution. It would, without question, defeat the objects for which Hampton and Tuskegee have persistently stood, and for which they have ever worked and are still very successfully working.

No one familiar with the curricula of these two schools would for a moment raise such a question. General Armstrong saw, as few people did, the moral and intellectual value of industrial training aside from its merely economic importance. He founded a school on an entirely different basis from any that had been known before—the basis of character-building through practical education, industrial training, and self-help.

During the thirty-six years of its history, Hampton has sent into the world about 1,200 gradutes and 5,000 undergraduates, many of whom have taken with them the spark that has started many other Hamptons, large and small, among the Negroes of the South and the Indians of the West. Hampton's success, and indeed the success of any institution, depends not so much upon the scholastic attainments of its pupils as upon the work that those who have received its instruction accomplish. Hampton glories, and justly, in the loyalty of its graduates and in the faithfulness with which they have inculcated and exemplified the traditions and principles for which it stands. Hampton glories in Tuskegee, because Tuskegee has started in so many communities the spark of true life and real civilization; in the impetus and inspiration it has given, so beautiful and so perfect a consummation of the prophetic vision of Hampton's founder.

Can the relations between the two institutions be better stated than in the words of their two

HAMPTON INSTITUTE

founders? After a visit to Tuskegee, General Armstrong said: " The Tuskegee school is a wonderful work and Mr. Washington is a remarkable man. He has carried out the idea of training the head, hand, and heart in a wonderfully complete and perfect way. This school is very much like the one at Hampton, and any one can recognize the similarity, but he has made many improvements. It is not merely an imitation. It is the Hampton Idea adapted and worked into a most sensible and efficient application to the needs of the Alabama Negroes." In the same memorial address at General Armstrong's funeral from which I quoted at the beginning of this paper, Mr. Washington said, " The rose I place on his grave is *his* work at Tuskegee."

Hampton and Tuskegee, striving along common lines for common ends, intimate in relationship, interdependent, each frankly criticizing and freely advising, each profiting by the failures of the other, each benefiting by the successes of the other, are both working as best they may toward that " far-off divine event to which the whole creation moves."

PART II

*AUTOBIOGRAPHIES BY
GRADUATES OF THE SCHOOL*

I

A COLLEGE PRESIDENT'S STORY

By Isaac Fisher

I was born January 18, 1877, on a plantation called Perry's place, in East Carroll Parish, Louisiana, and was the sixteenth and last child of my parents. My early childhood was uneventful, save during the year 1882, when, by reason of the breaking of the Mississippi River levee near my home, I was compelled, together with my parents, to live six months in the plantation cotton-gin, fed by the Federal Government and by the determination never to live so close to the "Big Muddy" again; and during 1886, in which year my mother died.

Up to this latter year my life had been nothing more than that of the average Negro boy on a cotton-farm. While I had been too young to feel the burden of farm-life toil, I had not been spared a realization of the narrowness and the dwarfing tendencies of the lives which the Negro farmers and their families were living, and, in my heart, I cursed the farm and all its environs as being in verity an inferno on earth. A broader knowledge of the causes which operated to produce the cheerless life against which my child-nature rebelled, and a clearer insight into the possibilities of rural life, have altered this early impression; and to-day I find myself thinking some thoughts relative to the life lived near to nature's heart which are not at all complimentary to the bustle and selfishness of city life.

The death of my mother furnished the opportunity to leave the farm and go to a city; and I took advantage of this, going to Vicksburg, Miss., to live with an older sister. I had always desired to go to school, and had spent four terms of six months each in the country school near my home; but for some reason, which I can not now remember, I attended the city school in Vicksburg but one year, after which I was employed as a cake-baker's assistant and bread-wagon driver. A short time before this I was a house-boy in the city. I was, at the time of my employment in the bakery, an omnivorous reader of the newspapers, and, in fact, of all kinds of literature; but my hours of labor at both places were so long and incessant that I found it almost impossible to do any reading during my employment at either place.

A COLLEGE PRESIDENT'S STORY

Finally I saw and took advantage of an opportunity to secure employment with the drug firm of W. H. Jones & Brother; and I count my work in this store, and with these gentlemen as employers, as the turning-point in my life, because there my work demanded some intelligence above the average. I had some chance to study, and in addition, when it was found by these white men that I loved to read, all magazines, newspapers, and drug journals, not needed by the firm and the physicians whose offices were with them, were given to me. I never make any mention of my life in Vicksburg without mentioning, in particular, Mr. W. H. Jones; for not only was he a kind and considerate employer, but I learned from his actions that a white man could be kind and interested in a Negro—a fact which no amount of reasoning could have driven into my stubborn understanding previous to that time.

There came a time when I learned that at the Tuskegee Institute, in Alabama, any poor Negro boy who was willing to work could pay for all his education in labor. To hear was to act. I wrote to Mr. Washington, asking if my information was correct. The affirmative answer came at once. It was the middle of August, and school

TUSKEGEE AND ITS PEOPLE

began in September, but I determined to be present at the opening of the school year. I was then a boy wearing short trousers, but I immediately set about preparing to deliver a "lecture" to help raise funds for my trip. With a knowledge of the subject, and an assurance which I have never since assumed, I spoke to a large audience in Vicksburg on the question, Will America Absorb the Negro? I settled the question then and there to my own satisfaction, even if I did not convince the nation that my affirmative conclusion was rational. The "lecture" netted me my fare to Tuskegee, with a few dollars over, and brought me from Rev. O. P. Ross, pastor of the African Methodist Episcopal Church in Vicksburg, the offer of a scholarship at Wilberforce College at the expense of his church. I respectfully declined the offer, feeling that I did not want to bind myself to any particular denomination by accepting so great a gift; but I have always felt very kindly toward that church ever since.

My first glimpse of Mr. Washington was had in the depot in Montgomery, Ala., where a friend and I, on our way to Tuskegee, had changed cars for the Tuskegee train. Two gentlemen came into the waiting-room where we were seated, one

A COLLEGE PRESIDENT'S STORY

a man of splendid appearance and address, the other a most ordinary appearing individual, we thought. The latter, addressing us, inquired our destination. Upon being told that we were going to Tuskegee, he remarked that he had heard that Tuskegee was a very hard place—a place where students were given too much work to do, and where the food was very simple and coarse. He was afraid we would not stay there three months. We assured him that we were not afraid of hard work, and meant to finish the course of study at Tuskegee at all hazards. He then left us. Very soon after, the gentleman who had so favorably impressed us, and whom we afterward found to be the capable treasurer of the Tuskegee Institute, Mr. Warren Logan, came back and told us that our interlocutor was none other than the President of the school to which we were going.

Arriving at Tuskegee, I found what it meant to be in a school without a penny, without assurance of help from the outside, and wholly dependent upon one's own resources and labor; and I found further that in the severe, trying process through which Mr. John H. Washington, superintendent of industries, brother of Mr. Booker T. Washington, and familiarly though very respectfully known to the students as "old man John," put all students who offered to work for their education, only the fittest, and the fittest of the fit at that, survived.

I was assigned work with the resident physician, a very efficient woman doctor from Philadelphia; and I have a recollection, by no means dim, that when this good woman made her monthly report to the treasurer, she could write, "Health Department to Isaac Fisher, Dr., $12.50—value received." Every morning before breakfast it was my duty to go to the rooms of six hundred young men to see if any were ill, have those who were, carried to the hospital, report all such to four departments, take meals to those confined in the hospital, attend to all their wants, keep their building heated and supplied with fuel, and— But space will not permit the full catalogue of duties. At the end of such a day's work I would attend the night-school during its session of two hours.

Desiring to learn a trade, I asked permission to enter the printing-office for the next year. This was not granted until it was found that I would not leave the school during the summer, but would remain and work until the beginning of the next school year. Accordingly, when my second year

A COLLEGE PRESIDENT'S STORY

began I entered the printing-office as an apprentice. During that year I suffered actual want and privation in the matter of shoes and clothes; but later came under the notice of Mrs. Booker T. Washington, who made arrangements by which I could procure some of the second-hand clothes and shoes sent from the North to the school for just such cases. At the end of this year my health, as a result of my work in the office, was so poor that the resident physician recommended my removal therefrom. To the surprise of Mr. J. H. Washington, I asked to be transferred to the farm; and I think I proved while working on the school-farm that I was sincere when I said that I would work wherever I was placed.

It was during this summer that Mr. Booker T. Washington showed me that I had come favorably under his notice. At one of the weekly prayer-meetings, conducted by the chaplain, Mr. Penney, and at which Mr. Washington was present, I made some remarks relative to the agnosticism of the late Col. Robert G. Ingersoll. The following day Mr. Washington sent for me, inquired my age and class in the school, and then said some very kind things about the talk which I had made in the prayer-meeting, and made me a conditional promise of his friendship, which, despite my oft-proven unworthiness, he has ever since given me in unstinted measure. After that second year my hardships as a "work-student" were practically over.

In my third year I entered the day-school, working one day in every week and every other Saturday, and going to school the remainder of the time. While the school made compulsory the earning of some money on the part of all students, it set no maximum limit on the amounts to be earned. I elected to earn as much as I could under the circumstances, earning, by reason of the many odd jobs which I did, often as much as $20 per month, going to school every day in the meantime. The average amount usually earned is $5 and $6 per month. At one time I worked eight days per month on the farm, sent notes of the school to 127 Negro newspapers, cleaned one laboratory every day, played in both the brass band and the orchestra, blew the bugle for the battalion, and taught two classes in the night-school, for each of which duties I received pay; and even though I broke down under the accumulated strain soon after my graduation, I carried my point and completed the course of study as I had planned.

THE CARNEGIE LIBRARY BUILDING.

A COLLEGE PRESIDENT'S STORY

In my fourth year I won the Trinity Church (Boston) Prize of $25 for oratory; and in my senior year won the Loughridge Book Prize for scholarship, and also the valedictory of my class, graduating in 1898.

I was immediately sent to the Schofield School, a Quaker institution for Negroes in Aiken, S. C., to organize farmers' conferences on the order of those conducted by the Tuskegee Institute, and to serve as a teacher in the school. After one year's service in that position Mr. Washington asked me to accept the position of Assistant Northern Financial Agent for Tuskegee. I accepted, and remained two years in New England, helping to interest friends in my *alma mater*. At my own request I was transferred from the Northern work to the South, being assigned this time to the Negro Conference work in Alabama. Before beginning this work I was married to a Tuskegee girl, Miss Sallie McCann.

Within a few months a principal was needed for the Swayne Public School of Montgomery, Ala., and this in the middle of the school year. Mr. Washington recommended me for the work, and I was elected to the position. At the close of the term I went to New York to study the public-school system of that city as far as possible. While there I was reelected principal of the Swayne School, and a notice of the election reached me one morning. Three hours later I received a letter from the secretary of the University of Arkansas (white) informing me that my name had been presented to the board of trustees of that institution, and I had been elected to the presidency of the State Branch Normal College at Pine Bluff, Ark. I was not a candidate for the position, but seeing in it an opportunity for greater usefulness, I accepted the position in my twenty-fifth year, and have just been reelected to serve a third term as president of the school. The Branch Normal College was established in 1875 as one of the Land Grant colleges, and has a property valuation of $100,000.

Over my desk hangs a picture of the Principal of Tuskegee; and in my desk are views of the institution which he has built. But these may be removed. In the book of my memory and in the secret chambers of my heart I have enshrined the two names which, with God and the parents now on the other side of the Great Divide, have shaped and given direction to my whole life—Tuskegee and Booker T. Washington.

II

A SCHOOL PRINCIPAL'S STORY

By William H. Holtzclaw

I was born in Randolph County, Ala., near the little town of Roanoke. The house in which I first saw the light—or that part of it which streamed through the cracks, for there were no windows—was a little log cabin 12 by 16 feet. I know very little of my ancestry, except that my mother was the daughter of her mother's master, born in the days of slavery, and up to 1864 herself the slave of her half-brother. She was born in the State of Georgia. My father was born in Elmore County, Ala. He never knew his father, but remembered his mother and eleven brothers. My mother was married twice before she married my father. She married first at the age of fifteen. I am the fifth of fifteen children, and my father's oldest child. Neither my father nor my mother could read or write; mother could get a little out of some pages of the Bible by spelling each word as she came to it.

TUSKEGEE AND ITS PEOPLE

My early years were spent on a farm. When only four years old I was put to such work as I could do—such as riding a deaf and blind mule, while my brother plowed him in order to make him go forward, for he cared nothing for assault from the rear. We worked for a white man for one-fourth of the crop. He furnished the stock, land, and seeds, and we did the work, although he was supposed to help. He furnished money to "run" us at fifteen to a hundred per cent, according to the time of the year. He grew wealthier; we grew, if possible, poorer. Before I was fifteen years old I instinctively felt the injustice of the scheme. When the crop was divided he got three loads of corn to our one, and somehow he always got all the cotton: never did a single bale come to us.

Those were hard times for us; for it must be remembered that this was in the days of reconstruction and the Ku-Klux-Klan, and if to this be added the fact that my father, a young and inexperienced man, had started out with a family of six on his hands, some idea of the situation may be had. I can recall having been without food many a day, and the pangs of hunger drove me almost to desperation. But mother and father

A SCHOOL PRINCIPAL'S STORY

would come late at night from a day of depressing toil and excruciating inward pain, the result of their inability to relieve our suffering, and pacify us for the night with such things as they had been able to get. When I awoke the next morning they were gone again on a food mission.

Hunger would sometimes nearly drive us mad. My brother and I were given a meal of pie-crusts from the white folks' table one day, and as we ate them, Old Buck, the family dog, who resembled an emaciated panther, stole one of the crusts. It was our dinner. We loved Old Buck, but we had to live first; so my brother lit on him, and a battle royal took place over that crust. Brother was losing ground, so I joined in, and, coming up from the rear, we conquered and saved the crust, but not till both of us were well scratched and bitten.

I was put to school at the age of six. Both mother and father were determined that their children should be educated. School lasted two months in the year—July and August. The schoolhouse was three miles from our house, but we walked every day, my oldest sister carrying me astride her neck when I gave out. Sometimes we had an ear of roasted green corn in our basket for dinner, or a roasted sweet potato, but more often simply persimmons, or fruit and nuts picked from our landlord's orchard and from the forest.

When cotton began to open, in the latter part of August, the landlord wanted us to stop school and pick cotton, and I can distinctly remember how my mother used to outgeneral him by slipping me off to school through the woods, following me through the swamps and dark places, with her hand on my back, shoving me on till I was well on the way, and then returning to try to do as much in the field that day as she and I together would be expected to do. When the landlord came to the quarters early to look for me, my mother would hide me behind the cook-pot and other vessels. When I was a little older I had to play my part on the farm. Mother now worked another scheme. I took turns with my brother at school and at the plow. What he learned at school on his school-day was taught to me at night, and vice versa. In this way we got a month of schooling each during the year, and got the habit of home study.

Our family was increasing rapidly, and to keep the children even roughly clothed and fed was about all that could be done under the circumstances. When the school exhibition took place and every girl was expected to have a white dress and

A SCHOOL PRINCIPAL'S STORY

every boy a pair of white pantaloons, my mother was often put to her trumps to get these things. Father would not trouble himself about them, as he said they were useless. But the teacher said they were necessary, and his word was law and gospel with most parents in our community. An exhibition was near at hand and three of us had no white pantaloons. Mother manipulated every scheme, but no cloth yet to make them! Finally the day arrived, but not till mother solved the problem by getting up before dawn that morning and making three pairs of white pantaloons for us out of her Sunday petticoat. Mother was of a determined disposition, and seldom failed to solve a domestic problem. We looked about as well as other people's children in that exhibition—at least we thought we did, and that was sufficient. But it must be remembered that there is just so much cloth, and no more, in a petticoat. So our suits were necessarily made tight. I had to be careful how I got around on the stage.

I usually had different teachers every year, as one teacher seldom cared to stay at a place for more than a session. I well remember the disadvantages of this custom. One teacher would have me in a Third Reader and fractions, another in

TUSKEGEE AND ITS PEOPLE

Fifth Reader and addition. When I reached the point where the teacher ordered me to get a United States History, the book-store did not have one, but sold me a biography of Martin Luther instead, which I studied for some time, thinking that I was learning something about the United States. I did not know what the United States was or was like, although I had studied geography and knew something about South America and Africa; and my teacher did not tell me. My teacher at this time was a good man, but that was all. Many of my teachers knew very little, but I thought they knew everything, and that was sufficient, for their teaching was wholesome. I remember one or two, however, whose work, under the circumstances, would be hard to match even now.

As soon as I was old enough I was hired out for wages, to help support the family. My school opportunities were now almost gone, and for this reason, together with a desire for more excitement, I began to grow restless on the farm. I grew morose. I pulled myself loose from all public functions, ceased to attend any public meetings, save regular monthly church meetings, and betook me to the woods, where I read everything I could get. It was during this time that accidentally, I

A SCHOOL PRINCIPAL'S STORY

may say providentially, I got hold of a book containing the life of Ignacius Sancho; and I have never read anything that has given me more inspiration. I wish every Negro boy in the land might read it. I read and worked, and helped to support the family. I had vowed that as soon as I was twenty-one I would leave for some school and there stay until I was educated. I was already a little in advance of the young people in my community, so I spent my long winter evenings teaching a little night-school to which the young people of the neighborhood came.

All my life up to this time my father had been working as a tenant. He now determined to strike out for himself—buy stock and rent land. The mule he bought soon became hopelessly lame in the back. It was a peculiar sort of illness. Once upon his feet, he could work all day without difficulty, but when he lay down at night he had to be helped up the following morning. During that entire season the first thing I heard each morning was the voice of my father, " Children, children, get up! let's go and help up the old mule." A neighbor also was called in each morning to help. Toward the end of the season the school opened. We were so anxious to enter, that we determined to help the old mule. My brother and I hitched ourselves to the plow, and sister did the plowing. Early each morning we plowed in this way, and soon finished the crop and entered the little school.

My father and some others had built a little school out of pine poles which they had cut, and hauled to the spot on their shoulders. The teacher, a married man, easily won all his pupils, but I could never forgive him for winning and finally eloping with his pretty assistant teacher.

Christmas eve, 1889, I went to bed a boy. Just after breakfast the next morning I became a man—my own man. "Sandy Claw" did not come that night, although I had hung up my stocking, and I was feeling bad about it. After breakfast my father called me out into the yard, where we seated ourselves on the protruding roots of a large oak-tree, and there he set me free.

"Son," said he, "you are nearing manhood, and you have no education; besides, if you remain with me I will not be able to help you when you are twenty-one. We've decided to make you free, if you'll make us one promise—that you will educate yourself."

By that time my mother had joined the party.

A SCHOOL PRINCIPAL'S STORY

I cried, I know not why, and my mother cried; even my father could not conceal his emotion. I accepted the proposal immediately, and although we usually took Christmas till New Year's day, my Christmas that year was then at an end. Manhood had dawned upon me that morning. I tried to be calm, but inwardly I was like a fish out of water.

I struck out to find work, that I might make money to go to school. One mile across the forest brought me to a man who hired me, and promised me $9.25 a month for nine months.

At the end of six months I came across the Tuskegee Student, published at the Tuskegee Normal and Industrial Institute. I read every line in it. On the first page was a note: " There is an opportunity for a limited number of able-bodied young men to enter the Tuskegee Normal and Industrial Institute and work their way through, provided application is made at once. Booker T. Washington, Principal."

Work their way through! I had never heard of such a thing before. Neither had I heard of Tuskegee. I sent in my application. I did not know how to address a letter, and so only put " Booker T. Washington " on the envelope. Somehow he received it and gave me permission to come.

TUSKEGEE AND ITS PEOPLE

There ensued a general scramble to get ready to go by the opening of school. I broke off relations with my employer by compromising for a suit of clothes and $8 in money. My chum, a man of about forty years of age, seeing the struggle I was making to get off, offered to help me, or rather to show me how to get the money easily by stealing a few chickens and selling them. It was a tempting bait, but against all the previous teachings of my mother. He argued, and my mother, who was not there, also argued within me. I could not consent. My friend pitied me and offered to do the job himself.

To get a supply of clothes to take to Tuskegee was the question. Up to that time I had never worn an undershirt, or a pair of drawers, or a stiff-bosom shirt, or a stiff collar. All these I had not only to get, but had to learn to wear them. My shirts and collars were bought second-hand from a white neighbor and were all too large by three numbers.

The last day of September, 1890, I left for Tuskegee. When I reached there, although I was a young man, I could not tell what county I lived in, in answer to Mr. Washington's question. I was admitted, after some hesitancy on the part

A SCHOOL PRINCIPAL'S STORY

of Principal Washington, and sent to the farm to work for one year in the daytime and to attend school at night.

I was dazed at the splendor of Tuskegee. There was Armstrong Hall, the most imposing brick structure I had ever seen. Then came Alabama Hall, where the girls lived. How wonderful! I could hardly believe that I was not dreaming, and I was almost afraid I should awake. When I went to bed that night I got between two sheets—something I had not been accustomed to do. About twelve o'clock an officer came in, threw the cover off me, and asked some questions about nightshirts, comb and brush, and tooth-brush, with all of which I was but meagerly acquainted. He made me get up, pull off my socks, necktie, collar, and shirt, and told me I would rest better without them. I didn't believe him, but I obeyed.

The next morning I saw more activity among Negroes than I had ever seen before in my life. Not only was everybody at work, but every soul seemed to be in earnest. I heard the ringing of the anvil, the click of machinery, the music of the carpenters' hammers. Before my eyes was a pair of big fat mules drawing a piece of new and improved farm machinery, which literally gutted the earth as the mules moved. Here was a herd of cattle, there a herd of swine; here thumped the mighty steam-engine that propelled the machine which delivered up its many thousand of brick daily; there was another machine, equally powerful, turning out thousands of feet of pine lumber every day. Then there were the class-rooms, with their dignified teachers and worthy-looking young men and women. Amid it all moved that wonderful figure, Booker T. Washington.

I began at once a new existence. I made a vow that I would educate myself there, or I would die and be buried in the school cemetery. When Mr. Washington stood at the altar in the first service which I attended and uttered a fervent prayer asking for guidance, and for spiritual and financial strength to carry on that great work, I felt that the Lord would surely answer his prayer. Since then I have traveled practically all over this country, and in one foreign country, without once seeing anything that made so deep an impression on me.

Simultaneously with this opportunity for self-education came many real hardships—to say nothing of imaginary hardships—which nearly resulted

MORNING AT THE BARNS ON THE SCHOOL FARM
Teams of horses and cattle ready to start for the day's work.

A SCHOOL PRINCIPAL'S STORY

disastrously to my health. I was poorly clad for the extraordinary winter then setting in. I had only one undershirt and one pair of drawers. I could not, of course, put these articles in the laundry, and therefore had to pull them off on Saturday nights, wash them, and get them dry enough to wear by breakfast on Sunday morning. It followed that many Sunday mornings found me sitting at the table wearing damp underwear. I could do no better, without leaving school, and this I was determined not to do. I was earnest in my work, and was promoted from a common laborer to be a hostler in charge of all boys dealing with horses, and then to the much-sought position of special assistant to the farm manager.

I was beginning to see the mistakes of my former life, the time I had lost, and now applied myself diligently. I carried a book with me everywhere I went, and not a second of time would I lose. While driving my mules with a load of wood, I would read until I reached the place of unloading. Mr. Washington took note of this, and upon one occasion, while admonishing the students to make good use of their time, said: " There is a young man on the grounds who will be heard from some day because of his intense application to study and diligence in his work." I listened. I knew he was speaking of me, and the fact that I was to be "heard from" later made me double my resolutions.

In September, 1891, I had to my credit in the treasury of the institution $100, and I was now ready to enter the day-school, to measure arms with the more fortunate students. But, alas! sickness overtook me, and when I emerged from the hospital, after about two months' sickness, my doctor's bill was exactly $100. My accumulated credit went to pay it.

This was the penalty for making the transit from a lower to a higher civilization. When I went without undergarments at home, my health was saved because of uniformity of habit. Now it was injured because I could wear them this week, but might not be able to do so the next—irregularity of habit. Then, too, Tuskegee gave me such living-rooms as I had never lived in, or hoped to. I had lived in log houses, which are self-ventilating. Now I had either overventilated or failed to ventilate my room. It is a difficult matter to make the transit from a lower to a higher civilization. There are many obstacles, and many have fallen by the way.

A SCHOOL PRINCIPAL'S STORY

I went home to recuperate, but returned to Tuskegee in a few weks, and as I had no money I was again permitted to enter the night-school and work during the day. This time I took up the printers' trade. Here I broke over the conventional rule of acting "devil" six months, and began setting type after one month in the office. In six months I was one of the school's regular compositors; and in one term I had sufficient credit with the treasurer to enter the day-school.

But I was not yet to enter. A letter came from my father, saying, "If you wish to see me again alive, I think it would be well to come at once." I went. My father died a few days after I got home, June 27, 1893.

All hope of future schooling seemed now at an end. My only concern was to do the best I could with the exceedingly heavy load now left on my hands. I pulled off my school-clothes, went to the field, and finished the crop father had left. There was a heavy debt, and I began to teach school to pay this debt. Of course I knew very little, but I taught what I knew—and, I suppose, some things I didn't know.

I think even now that I did the people some good. I had not learned much at Tuskegee in

TUSKEGEE AND ITS PEOPLE

books, but I had learned much from Mr. Washington's Sunday evening talks in the chapel. I had listened carefully to him and had treasured up in my heart what he had said from time to time. Now I was teaching it to others. I felt I was to this little community what Mr. Washington was to Tuskegee. So I made the people whitewash their fences and fix up their houses and premises generally. They were very poor, and when the school closed they could not pay me. I told them I would take corn, peas, potatoes, sirup, pork, shucks, cotton-seed—in fact, anything with which they wished to pay me.

Wagons were secured and loaded, and for several days all sorts of provisions were hauled to my mother's house and stored away for winter. I went to the house of one good widow, who said:

" 'Fesser, I ain't got nothin' to pay you wid but dis 'ere house-cat, and he's a good'n. I owes you twenty-five cents, and I wants to pay it. You done my little gal good—more'n any teacher ever did. She ain't stop' washin' her face yit when she gits up in de mornin'."

"Very well," I said, "I'll take the cat with thanks and call the debt square."

Another said: " 'Fesser, I heard you was com-

A SCHOOL PRINCIPAL'S STORY

ing, and I hid all my meat in de smoke-house, and says: 'I'll tell him I ain't got none;' but when I seed you coming I tole de chillen to go open de smoke-house. Anybody who do my chillens as much good as you, can get every bit de meat I got." From that woman I got fifty pounds of meat.

Another good woman wanted me to take her only pair of scissors, and when I refused to do so, she put them into my coat-pocket, saying the man who taught her child so much must be paid.

For three years I taught school with one personal object in view—the support of my mother and her family. Mother was not satisfied with this; she wanted me educated. Finally she married again, for no higher reason than to permit me, and the other children growing up, to go to school. My hope for an education was again renewed, and I went back to Tuskegee.

Nearly everybody had forgotten that I had ever been there. Notwithstanding I had been out nearly three terms, I had kept pace with my class, making one class each year, the same as if I had been in school. Upon a very critical examination, in which I averaged ninety-three for all subjects, I entered the B Middle class in the day-school.

Financially I was very little better off than

when I left, but I had learned how to manipulate things in such a way as to make it possible to remain in school. I knew a trade at which I could easily make a dollar a day in credit, and I could teach during the vacation. Things went smoothly for one year. Then my brother came, and I had to support him in part. Just about the time I was getting myself adjusted to this, my sister came. I knew I should have to support her almost wholly, so I felt like giving up under such a triple burden; but I held on. I had to deny myself many of the pleasures of school life in order to make two ends meet. I had to wear two pairs of pantaloons and one pair of drawers; and I remember one Sunday, while the school was enjoying a good sermon by a great bishop, I was in the shop melting some glue, with which I glued patches on my only pair of pantaloons, which had reached a condition where thread would no longer hold the patches on. I will not tell what happened when the patches had been on for a few days.

But amid all these conflicting affairs of my school-days ran an immense amount of pleasure, more than I had ever known before. I was gradually coming to see things as they are in the affairs of men. I thought then, and I still think, that

A SCHOOL PRINCIPAL'S STORY

no sacrifice was too great when there was such a golden opportunity. To sit and listen to one Sunday evening talk by Principal Washington was worth all the trouble one had to undergo for a year.

Two years before I graduated I began to inquire what I was made for—what calling should I follow? It was hard to decide. Mr. Washington's teaching had impressed me that I should do something to help those less fortunate than myself, and that in the very darkest place I could find. My father had called me to his death-bed and said to me: "Son, I want you to become a teacher of your people. I have done what I could in that direction. The people need your services." I recalled how in his last moments I had promised him I would carry out his wishes. There was nothing else left for me to do but to go into those dark places. But there was the rub; and every Sunday evening Mr. Washington thundered that same theme: "Go into the darkest places, the places where you are most needed, and there give your life with little thought of self." I knew about those dark places. I had been born in one of them. I had been spending my vacations teaching in them.

Once, while teaching in the State of Georgia,

TUSKEGEE AND ITS PEOPLE

I boarded with a family where there were fifteen besides myself, all sleeping, eating, and cooking in the same room. There were three young women in the family. When bedtime came I had to go out of doors and amuse myself with the stars till all the women were in bed; then they would extinguish the hearth-light by putting some ashes on it and let me come in and go to bed. I had to keep my head under the cover the next morning while they got up and dressed. I used to sleep with my nose near a crack in the wall in order to get fresh air. One little girl in the family, while saying her prayers one night, begged the Lord to let the angels come down and stay with them that night. Her little brother promptly interrupted her by saying that she ought to have sense enough to know that there was no room in that bed for angels, as there were already five persons in it. I was used to the country and its worst conditions. I prayed over the matter till finally I gave myself, heart and mind, to whatever place should call me.

During my last year at Tuskegee I was made a substitute salaried teacher in the night-school. My financial burdens were now lifted and my school life became one great pleasure. Toward the

A SCHOOL PRINCIPAL'S STORY

end of my Senior year I decided to try for the Trinity Prize of $25 for the best original oration. I remembered what Mr. Washington had so often said: that a man usually gets out of a thing what he puts into it. I determined to put $100 worth of effort into this contest. I was awarded the prize.

A place was offered to me at Tuskegee as academic teacher, but I declined it. I had settled in my mind that I would go to the State of Mississippi, which I had found by two years of investigation was the place where my services were most needed. I could not go to Mississippi at once. I had not money to pay my way, so I accepted a position with my friend, William J. Edwards, at his school in Snow Hill, Ala., where I worked for four years, never losing sight of my Mississippi object. While at Snow Hill I married Miss Mary Ella Patterson, a Tuskegee graduate of the Class of '95. We put our earnings together and built us a comfortable little home. One child, William Sidney, was born to us, but lived only six months.

It took me just two years to convince my wife that there was any wisdom or judgment in leaving our little home and going to Mississippi, where neither of us was known. But finally she gave herself, soul and body, to my way of thinking.

TUSKEGEE AND ITS PEOPLE

The way was now clear for me to make the start. Just before I left for Mississippi, one of my old teachers from Tuskegee visited me. He inquired about my going to Mississippi, and when I explained the scheme to him, he said jestingly, "You know there is no God in Mississippi." I simply replied that then I would take "the one that Alabama had" with me.

I could not take my wife, for she was under the care of a physician at that time. I decided to leave nearly all my ready cash with her. I did not take quite enough for my railroad fare, for I had expected to sell my wife's bicycle when I reached Selma, the nearest town, and thus secure enough money to finish my trip. But when I got to Selma the wheel would not sell, so I boarded the train without money enough to reach Utica, the place in Mississippi to which I was bound.

I had not got far into the State of Mississippi when my purse was empty. I stopped off at a little town, late at night, where there were no boarding-houses, and no one would admit me to a private house to sleep. I wandered about until I came upon an old guano-house, and crawled into this and slept until the break of day. Then I crawled out, pulled myself together, jumped

A SCHOOL PRINCIPAL'S STORY

astride my bicycle, and made my way toward Utica, through a wild and unfrequented part of Mississippi. But before I could reach Utica my wheel broke down, whereupon I put it upon my shoulder, rolled up my trousers, and continued the journey to Utica. I soon met a young man who relieved me of my burden by trading me his brass watch for the wheel and giving me $2 to boot.

I had previously got myself elected principal of the little county school, which, if I could pass the State examination, would pay me a little salary, which would be a great help to me while I worked up the Industrial and Normal School which I had come to build. Much depended on my ability to pass the examination. Tuskegee's reputation was at stake—my own reputation was at stake; for, if I failed, the people would certainly lose confidence in me, and make it impossible for me to accomplish my purpose.

I was out of money, and this was the only way I could see to get any for a long time. If I failed, my wife—who was still in Alabama, and who believed in my ability to do anything—would perhaps lose respect for me, and, most of all, the failure to pass the examination might upset all my plans and blast all my hopes. I confess I went to that examination with a sort of anxious determination. I did not, however, find it half so difficult as I had expected. I soon succeeded in obtaining the necessary license to teach in the public schools of the State.

The little schoolhouse where the school had been heretofore was so much out of repair that we could not risk having pupils under its roof. I had hoped to open in the church, but the good deacons would not permit this. So the few pupils who came the first day were gathered together under an oak-tree, and there were taught. After some time a temporary cabin was fixed up, and in this we taught the entire winter. The cabin was practically no protection against the rain, and less against the winter winds. The wind literally came through from all directions—from the sides, ends, above, and beneath.

We soon had the floor stopped up with clay. This brought about another disadvantage: when it began to rain through the roof, the water would collect on the floor until it was two or three inches deep. Two young women were helping me to teach. They often amused me by trying to maintain their dignity and keep out of the water at the same time. They would stand upon stools and fire questions at their pupils, who were standing

A SCHOOL PRINCIPAL'S STORY

in the water below while answering them. On such days as this I usually wore my overcoat and rubber shoes. I would then stand in the water and teach with as much indifference as possible. We bored holes in the floor to let the water out, but it usually came through the roof faster than it could escape. There was much suffering at this time on the part of both teachers and students, but it was all a joy and pleasure to me, for I felt that I had found my life-work.

I was a stranger to the people, and they had very little confidence in me. Some of them questioned my motives in every direction. At the first meeting of the patrons for the purpose of raising money, seventy-five cents were collected and were turned over to me to hold. In a couple of days some one demanded that the collection be taken out of my hands. I quietly turned it over to them. Then they got up a scramble as to which one should hold it. They settled the quarrel by selecting a white man in the town of Utica, in whom all of them had confidence. I then went out canvassing and got $10, which I promptly turned over. Immediately they wanted to turn it back to me to hold, together with what the white man had. They never again questioned my sincerity.

TUSKEGEE AND ITS PEOPLE

My wife, who was still in Alabama, kept writing me to let her join me. Explanations would do no good. She laid aside all the comforts of home life and came to live in a hovel. We rented a little room, bought a skillet and a frying-pan, a bed and two chairs, and set up housekeeping. I did the cooking, for my wife was a city girl and did not know how to cook on the open fireplace. We never contrasted our condition in Mississippi with that in Alabama; we simply made the best of what we had.

At first there was difficulty in securing land for a location, and many of the patrons began to feel that nothing would be accomplished. To offset this idea I purchased lumber for a building, had it put in the churchyard, and cut up ready for framing. The enthusiasm had to be kept up. Land was soon bought and the building started. Everybody felt now that something was going to be done. At the end of the first year's work I was able to make to the trustees a creditable report, from which the following is taken:

As soon as we secured a cabin to teach in, the young people came in great numbers. We soon had an attendance of 200. One teacher after an-

A SCHOOL PRINCIPAL'S STORY

other was employed to assist, until seven teachers were daily at work. After three months in our temporary quarters conditions were very trying. There was no money to pay teachers or to meet the grocery bills for teachers' board. The winter was well on, and the structure in which we were located was little protection against it. The rain easily came through the roof, and water was often two inches deep on certain parts of the floor. Several teachers and students were suffering with pneumonia or kindred disorders, as a result of all this exposure. I confess that during this dark period only a carefully planned system and much determination prevented despair.

During all this time I was trying to secure the interest of the people. I went from door to door, explaining our efforts; then I made a tour of the churches; after riding or walking five or ten miles at night I would return, and then teach the next day. After a protracted struggle of this kind, and after visiting almost everybody for many miles, I found that I had secured about $600. This greatly relieved us. Forty acres of land were purchased, and a part of the lumber for a good, comfortable building was put upon the grounds. Some of our trustees in New York city and Boston now came to our assistance, and with this, and contributions from a few other friends, we were able to get through the year. Although it was a great struggle, I found in it some pleasure.

TUSKEGEE AND ITS PEOPLE

To know that you were doing the work that the world needs, and must have done, is a pleasure even under trying difficulties.

Starting last October without a cent, in the open air, we have succeeded in establishing a regularly organized institution incorporated under the laws of the State of Mississippi, with 225 students and seven teachers, and with property valued at $4,000. Forty acres of good farm-land about a mile from town have been secured. A model crop is now growing on this farm. We have erected a building—a two-story frame—at a cost of something over $2,000.

I hope you will not get, from what I have said, an idea that I am measuring the success of my efforts by material advancement. I am not. There are forces which our labors have set to work here, the results of which can not be measured in facts and figures. One year ago religious services were held once a month, at which time the day was spent in singing, praying, and shouting. The way some of the people lived for the next twenty-nine days would shock a sensitive individual to read about it. Young people would gamble with the dice, etc., in a most despicable way, within a short distance of the church, during services; others would discharge revolvers at the church door during services; ignorance, superstition, vice, and immorality were everywhere present, notwithstanding the handful of determined Christian men and

A SCHOOL PRINCIPAL'S STORY

women who were trying to overcome these evil tendencies. I do not maintain that these evils have been crushed out. They have not. But what I do maintain is that the general current has been checked. The revolution is on; and if we continue the work here, as we surely will, these evil tendencies will soon be crushed out.

During this year the people themselves furnished $1,000 toward the support of the school. They have never before spent a tenth as much for education. The second year eleven teachers were employed and 400 students were admitted. The cost of operations was $10,000, all of which was raised during the year. We are now entering into our third term. Fifteen teachers have been employed, and the expenses of operation will be about $15,000, all of which I must raise by direct effort. Our property, all deeded to a board of trustees, is valued at $10,000.

I can not feel that I have accomplished much here in Mississippi, because I see all around me so much to be done—so much that I can not touch because of lack of means. But, being in the work to stay, I may, in the end, contribute my share to the betterment of man. If I have suffered much to build up this work, I can not feel that it is

TUSKEGEE AND ITS PEOPLE

a sacrifice. It is a colossal opportunity. The greater the sacrifice, the more extensive the opportunity. Whatever may have been accomplished already is certainly due more to my wife's superior judgment than to my own activity. Whatever I have been able to do myself here in Mississippi for my people has been due, first, to the teachings of my mother, and, second, to the all-important life-example and matchless teachings of Booker T. Washington.

III

A LAWYER'S STORY

By George W. Lovejoy

I can give no accurate date as to my birth, as my mother was a slave and thus it was not recorded, but I think I was born in the month of February, 1859. I was born in Coosa, one of the middle counties of Alabama.

I am the third child and the second son of eleven children, seven of whom are still living.

My father I do not remember, as he died when I was very young, but I most vividly remember my stepfather, the only father I ever knew.

Childhood to me was not that long season of " painless play " of which Whittier so beautifully sings, but I do remember that I was early impressed that my feet must have been made for the express purpose of treading " the mills of toil." When seven years of age my stepfather put a hoe in my little hands and bade me go and help my mother weed the cotton-patch, and from that day to the present time I have been constant in my application to some form of labor.

When my mind reverts to that early period of my life I become my own photographer and get various pictures of myself, either as picking, hoeing, or planting cotton, of pulling fodder or splitting rails, for these were the things I did from childhood to manhood.

My stepfather had been the foreman, or "driver," for his master when he was a slave, and I am persuaded to believe that he must have been an excellent one, for I can not remember in all my life when a day's work had been so full, so complete, so well done, that he would not press for a little more the next day.

Mortgaging of crops was then in vogue, as it is to-day, and my mind revolts when I think of how my young life and the lives of my mother, sisters, and brothers were burdened with the constant grind of trying to eke out a living and, if possible, get even a little ahead.

Some years, when conditions had been favorable, we were able to clear ourselves of debt and begin anew. But, seemingly, this prosperity was not for us, for these years of plenty were almost invariably followed by one or two less fruitful ones that came and "swallowed up the whole," leaving us as forlorn and as wretchedly poor as we were before. This failure of the crops because of drouths unduly long, wet seasons, the ravages of worms, caterpillars, and other uncontrollable circumstances, not only meant that the whole of that year's labor was to bring no tangible rewards, but that much property accumulated in more prosperous times was to be dissipated as well. I can recall repeated instances when all of my stepfather's live stock was taken for debt under this crushing system. And thus it was that my stepfather, and my mother, and the rest of the farmers for miles around existed!

During all these years my brothers, sisters, and myself were growing up in ignorance. Until I was ten years old I had never heard of a school for colored children. Even after the privilege of attending school two months of the year—July and August—had been accorded me, I am certain that the instruction received was of that kind that hinders more than it helps. Year after year the course of study would be repeated. Perhaps this repetition was necessary for more than one reason:

First, ten months' vacation does not tend to

firmly impress upon one's mind the knowledge acquired in two.

Second, the teachers themselves had such limited knowledge that two months were ample time in which to exhaust their store of knowledge, and, as examinations were so easy, it was not imperative that they do more than "keep school."

I remember quite distinctly that when I did go to school we used the proverbial Webster's blue-back speller. The majority of the pupils began with the "A, B, C," the alphabet, and went as far as "horseback," while apt pupils might be able to reach "compressibility." And so for years we went from "A" to "compressibility" on "horseback."

In those days the three "R's" were not confounded. Only one of them was given to us, and that in broken doses, for I reached manhood without being able to write a single word or to work a problem in mathematics.

Neither my mother nor stepfather could read or write a line; not a book, newspaper, or magazine was ever seen in our home. It was most unusual to see a colored man or woman who could either read or write.

When a mere boy I inwardly protested against

A LAWYER'S STORY

this manner of bringing-up. I determined to make my life more useful, to make it better than it was. But how long these years were! However, the day came when I was twenty-one, and I began to create a " life " for myself.

I immediately went to work doing farm labor, and saved my earnings until I had twenty-five or thirty dollars ahead. I then decided to go to school somewhere and to learn something. I found my first opportunity in Montgomery, Ala. I went there in November, 1883, and entered the Swayne School.

Everything was new and strange to me. I had never seen so large a schoolhouse before. I was dazed, bewildered. There I was, a great, grown man, in the class with little children, who looked upon me as a curiosity, something to be wondered at. I, too, looked at them with amazement, for it seemed next to impossible for young boys and girls to know as much as they seemed to know.

I can not say that I was heartily received by the pupils. I was awkward, and I discovered that the city children did not find me pleasingly companionable.

It is probable that at this point I should have

grown discouraged and given up had I not met that great and good man, Rev. Robert C. Bedford, who is now, as he has been for many years, secretary of the board of trustees of the Tuskegee Institute, and who travels among and reports upon the work of Tuskegee graduates and former students, but who was at that time pastor of the First Congregational Church in Montgomery. I regularly attended his church and the Sunday-school connected therewith, and received such help and encouragement from him as but few men can impart to others.

It was he who first told me of Tuskegee and advised me to enter there. I felt that this advice, if heeded, would work for my good. I was admitted to Tuskegee for the session beginning September, 1884, three years after the school had been opened.

When I entered Tuskegee I was filled with loathing for all forms of manual labor. I had been a slave to toil all my life and had resolved that, if it were possible for a colored man to make a living by doing something besides farming, splitting rails, or picking and hoeing cotton, I would be one of that number. I was compelled at the school, however, like the others, to work at some

STUDENTS PRUNING PEACH-TREES.

A LAWYER'S STORY

industry. I did some work on the farm and was one of the school's " boss " janitors.

Though I had no real inclination to learn a trade or to perform any kind of manual toil, I did desire to be useful, and throughout my whole school life at Tuskegee I had visions of myself seated in an office pondering over Blackstone, Kent, and Storey, with a " shingle " on the outside announcing my profession to all passers-by.

After spending some time in Tuskegee and diligently applying myself, I was much gratified to find that I was able to pass the State examination for a second-grade certificate, and to teach, during the vacation period, the very school in which I had so long before learned to spell " horseback " and " compressibility."

I spent four years in the Tuskegee Institute, graduating with the class of 1888.

Before graduating, I divulged to Mr. Washington my long-cherished ambition, and was somewhat chagrined to find that he did not think much of my dreams. He apparently sympathized with this larger vision, but seemed to think I ought to have more education. I suspect he was right. However, I was determined to make an effort to realize my ambitions. I insisted that he must help me to find a place to read law. After a while it was decided that I should begin in the office of Mr. William M. Reid, of Portsmouth, Va.

With this end in view, I taught in the State of Alabama from May, 1888, until April, 1889. I then left for Portsmouth.

Though I had worked for eleven months, I had but $1.25 when I reached Portsmouth. My salary had been meager, I had paid every cent I owed the school, and had met the many obligations necessary to living in a decently comfortable manner.

I found Mr. Reid to be an intelligent, studious, hard-working young man, with a fairly good practise, and in that hour of uncertainty and embarrassment he proved himself to be "the friend in need." With his aid I was not long in finding work by which I earned enough to pay my board and buy books to help me in my study of law at night.

I worked during the daytime at the United States Navy-Yard in Portsmouth, receiving $1.25 per day. I had never before earned so much money. I was able not only to meet my regular bills but to save something, and soon began to

A LAWYER'S STORY

collect a law library. I worked at the Navy-Yard for three years. It was my privilege to work upon the second-class battleship Texas, and upon the steel-protected cruiser Raleigh, both of which rendered admirable service in the Spanish-American War.

In the spring of 1892 I felt that I had sufficient knowledge of law to begin practising. I left Virginia and returned to Alabama. The tug of war had now begun. I found it exceedingly difficult to get examined. After trying for five months, I succeeded in getting a lawyer, a Mr. Thompson, of Macon County, Ala., to recommend me to the chancery court of that county for examination. I was examined in open court before all the practising attorneys of that bar, and was given license to practise law in the State of Alabama.

I was elated, overjoyed—my dream was nearing its realization!

I selected Mobile, Ala., a city of about fifty thousand inhabitants, as my field of labor. I opened my office on September 8, 1892, and have practised law there from that time to the present date. Though I have met many obstacles and have had many difficulties to surmount, I have never had to close my office, or seek other employment to make a living. I have done well.

I have experienced no embarrassment because of prejudice. The judges and juries have discussed cases with me in the same manner that they would with any other lawyer at the bar. I have even had a few white clients.

To get the confidence of my own people is the hardest problem I have had to solve, for I find that men are still sometimes without honor in their own country.

I am daily confronted with many petty difficulties. I sometimes find that even a religious difference will come between me and a probable client. Some think I should be a Baptist, others would have me a Methodist, and others still suggest that I should embrace the Catholic faith. I should also belong to every secret society in the city, and attend every public gathering no matter what the hour, whether it be called at high noon or at dawn of day.

Despite these things to be expected of a people but forty years free, and used to white judges, and juries, and lawyers, and unused to dealing with one of their own, I feel that I am still winning my way. It is my desire to help my fellow men,

A LAWYER'S STORY

and in return receive an appreciable share of their help.

After practising my profession for nearly two years, I was married to Miss Sarah E. Ogden, who was at that time a student at the Tuskegee Institute. We have been happily married for ten years and have been blessed with six children, only three of whom, I am sorry to state, are living.

I feel that I can not close this short sketch without paying a closing tribute to my *alma mater*—Tuskegee. Those lessons of thrift, industry, and integrity dwelt upon by Principal Washington and his coworkers, I shall never forget. My heart thrills and its pulses beat whenever I think of what it has meant to me to come in contact with the quickening influences of that school.

I lift up my voice and call her blessed, my Tuskegee!

IV

A SCHOOL TREASURER'S STORY

By Martin A. Menafee

I was born on a plantation in Lee County, Ala., and, as my parents were very poor, I was placed in the field and did not see the inside of a schoolroom until I was twelve years old. I then had a chance to attend a three months' school for six months, or for two years, as we usually called it. Before this I had had one of my shoulders dislocated through an accident and have been able to use but one arm since.

At this period I made up my mind to secure an education, and a gentleman who was teaching school at my home took me to an Alabama college, thinking that he could perhaps get me in school there. I told the president of the college that I wanted an education, and offered him my services in return for such opportunities as he would open to me, but seeing my condition, he soon concluded that I could render but little in the way of services.

A SCHOOL TREASURER'S STORY

I pleaded with him for a trial, but he refused me admittance, albeit in a very nice and polite manner.

I returned home, then at Oakbowery, Ala. Very soon after my return I heard of the Tuskegee Institute, and I think it was in July of that year when I made up my mind that I would start for this school, which was about forty miles from where I lived. After walking to Auburn, Ala., twelve miles, I waited for the train and, as she glided up, I walked in and took my seat. Before I left home I knew some walking would be necessary, and preferred doing it at the beginning of the journey. I was admitted on my arrival, after some parleying, and was promptly assigned to work in the brick-yard. After I had been there for two days I found that the sun had no pity on, or patience with, me; it seemed to blister me through and through. I finally concluded that the sun, together with the brick-yard, was blasting the hopes I had entertained and the determination I had fostered, of securing an education. I tried to get my work changed, but the Director of Industries did not see it as I did, and would not do it.

The next thing that I settled upon for relief was to get sick, but a day's trial of that showed that would not work. I decided that I would return home, where I was sure I would at least find no brick-yard to harass or disturb. My stay at the school was just about seven or eight days. I would like to add just here, however, that I am very glad that I was put on the brick-yard, as it certainly left in me the spirit of work after I got over that first affliction of heat.

Very soon after I had returned home I received a letter from one of the teachers of Talladega College, a Miss S. J. Elder, who met me when I was there seeking entrance, asking me to go to Jenifer, Ala., and attend a school there conducted by two white ladies; she said she would "foot" all of my bills. This greatly relieved me, and I considered it a great thing. Very soon thereafter I had my clothes ready, and was at Jenifer. I was there for one year, but Tuskegee was constantly on my mind; in fact, I had made up my mind to give it a second trial.

On October 29, 1894, I again went to Tuskegee and asked for admission. I was admitted with the understanding that I should stand up in the Chapel and make a public acknowledgment of the wrong I had done in leaving the school without permission. This seemed like a great humiliation, as I could hardly talk to one person, to say nothing

A SCHOOL TREASURER'S STORY

of the thousand students and teachers then there, as I stammered so much. Mr. Washington seemed to understand the situation and was kind enough to help me out by asking questions.

I was given work on the farm, and started out again with renewed vigor and determination to complete a course of study. The farm manager, Mr. C. W. Greene, was very kind to me and gave me work that I could do. After I had been on the farm about two weeks he placed me at the gates to keep out the cows and hogs that might be tempted to walk in on the school-lawns. This work I enjoyed, and very soon established an " office " under a tree near the gate. I held this position and kept this " office " for two years.

I was then taken from there and placed in Mr. Greene's office to help him. It was at Tuskegee that I first saw a typewriter and shorthand writing. I made up my mind that I would be a stenographer and typewriter, and thought that if I could learn this, that would be as high up as I cared to go in life. I borrowed a book on shorthand, not being able to purchase one, and began the study without a teacher. Very soon I realized that I had learned a little, and my ambition grew. I wanted a typewriter.

TUSKEGEE AND ITS PEOPLE

I got up enough courage to go to the Rev. R. C. Bedford, who often visited the school, and who was one of my best friends, and, in fact, is largely responsible for my being able to stay at Tuskegee as long as I did, and told him I wanted a typewriter; I repeatedly told him that my success in life largely depended upon my securing it. Mr. Bedford said he would see what could be done, and, in a very short time, he came from the North and brought the machine. When he informed me that he had brought it, it did seem that I could not stay on the grounds. I felt then that I had all that was necessary to make me a stenographer, and very soon declared myself a member of the stenographic world.

I advanced very well in these new studies and was given some work to do in the offices. The regular school stenographers helped me all they could.

The saddest experience I ever had in connection with the Tuskegee Institute was at the end of my second summer. I was very anxious to remain in the employ of the school, as my people were very poor and I did not care to be home on them unless I could become a full field hand, and I felt that the school had much work that I could do.

A SCHOOL TREASURER'S STORY

I appealed to the Director more than once to let me remain, but he replied each time that the work department was closed; that he could not take any more, and furthermore, that it was best that I return home. Mr. Bedford encouraged me all he could and told me that I might find something to do; that I should launch out for myself. I went to Opelika, and Mr. Bedford was on the same train. He and I were in Opelika together for about a half day. He was on his way to Beloit, Wis., his home, and I was on my way home to Oakbowery. About thirty minutes before it was time for my train to leave, I noticed a man who was very busy superintending the hauling of some lumber. This man asked my name, what I could do, and where I was from. For a moment I hesitated to tell him, but finally did. I found that he was the principal of the colored city school at Opelika, Professor J. R. Savage. Mr. Savage proved to be a true friend. He gave me work at once in the Summer Normal School he was conducting. I went to my home that evening, rejoicing that I had found work. When I returned to Opelika Mr. Savage asked me to take charge of the business department of the Summer Normal and teach shorthand and typewriting. I worked with him in this way for three summers, my vacation periods, with much success. We worked well together and in perfect harmony.

At the opening of each school year at Tuskegee I would be among the first to get there to begin my studies. I found that, in order to remain at Tuskegee, students had to have a real purpose. I had one, and I think so impressed the Faculty before leaving there.

I did not have all smooth sailing, and, at times, I would all but give up.

I was at Tuskegee for six years, and I recall those years with much pleasure and satisfaction. During my stay there I made many friends, and I can not refrain from mentioning the Rev. R. C. Bedford, who has helped me in so many ways; Mr. Warren Logan, the Treasurer of the school; Mrs. F. B. Thornton, the Matron, who took me as her son, and my dear friend, the farm manager, Mr. C. W. Greene. Many others were also very kind to me.

I completed my course of study in 1900. By this time Mr. Bedford had secured a position for me at Denmark, S. C., as stenographer to the principal, Miss Elizabeth E. Wright, a Tuskegee graduate. I did not hold this position very long

A SCHOOL TREASURER'S STORY

before it was decided in a meeting of the board of trustees to have me act as the school's treasurer. On being asked to take this place, I answered that I would do my best. I have now been here since the fall of the year of my graduation. I like the work immensely.

A word about the school: It is known as the Voorhees Industrial School, and is located in the midst of an overshadowing Negro population. It has just completed the seventh year of its existence. Miss Wright, the principal, founded it on faith. She is a delightfully spiritual woman, and was at first greatly opposed in her efforts by both the black and white people of this section. She persevered, however, and all the people are now her friends. Her work here has been but little short of marvelous. The pride of the grounds is a splendidly arranged Central Building, which cost $3,000. It contains offices, class-rooms, and a chapel that will seat 600 persons. A large building for girls, costing $4,000, has also been erected. A Tuskegee graduate drew the plans for both of these buildings. A barn which cost $800 we have also been able to complete, and are now using.

In our Faculty, in addition to Miss Wright, who is of the Class of 1904, Tuskegee Institute, we have six other Tuskegee graduates: a farm superintendent, a carpenter, a teacher of drawing, a principal of the primary department, a sewing and cooking teacher, a millinery teacher and industrial helper, and a treasurer and bookkeeper, myself.

The day- and boarding-pupils number 300.

Voorhees is one of the sixteen larger "offshoots" of Tuskegee Institute, manned and controlled by Tuskegee graduates. It is a chartered State institution, and has on its board of trustees white and colored persons, Northern and Southern. One of its very best and most helpful supporters and friends is a Southern white man who has helped it in ways innumerable, and has backed it when the courage of all of us has all but faltered.

By precept and example the school is helping the black masses of rural South Carolina to help themselves. The work we do is far different from that done by any other school in the State; we provide the way for our students, as at Tuskegee, because of their poverty, to work on the farm and in the shops during the day and attend school at night. Without this help most of them would be without any chance to attend school. Our students are

A SCHOOL TREASURER'S STORY

learning to dignify labor. None have yet graduated, as our school is young and most of those who come to us can not read or write a word. They are wofully ignorant, but so willing to learn, so earnest, and so persevering.

During the last school year, 1903–'04, we received from all sources $18,310.43. This will give some idea as to the scope and importance of our work, and of my work in disbursing this large sum as the treasurer of the school.

Our present property valuation is $25,000, and consists of 300 acres of land, 3 large buildings, a large barn, a schoolhouse for primary children, 4 cottages, an industrial building, 10 mules, 6 horses, 30 cows, 3 wagons, 3 buggies, etc., all free from indebtedness of any character. We stay out of debt; that for which we can not pay we do without.

We afford instruction in the following industries: Farming in its various branches, shoemaking, carpentry, cooking, sewing, housekeeping, laundering, millinery in a small way, printing, and blacksmithing.

The training received at Tuskegee has been of so much help to me since leaving there. I made up my mind after graduation that I would urge my parents and relatives to cease paying five and six bales of cotton each year for rent, and instead take the same amount of cotton and buy a place of their own. I am glad to say, through my efforts in this regard, they have been placed on a tract of 160 acres of good land, and it is practically paid for, they paying four bales of cotton a year. They are doing well and are making something for themselves. This project seemed a little strange to them for the first two years, but they are now used to it.

"He that hath a trade," saith Franklin, "hath an estate, and he that hath a calling, hath a place and honor." Since being out in the world I have learned not to wait for a higher position or a better salary, and have steadily sought to enlarge the ones I have had. I have tried to fill such positions as I have had as they were never filled before, by doing better work, by being more prompt, by being more thorough, more polite, and, in fact, I have filled them so completely that no one else could slip in by me. I have always laid great stress on work as a means of developing power; I am called by some of my friends a fanatic on this subject. My experience at Tuskegee taught me that our racial salvation is to come through hard, ear-

A SCHOOL TREASURER'S STORY

nest, intelligent, sincere work. I owe a world of gratitude to the Tuskegee Institute for the training I received there and for the great work it is doing for the Negro people.

I repeat, if I accomplish anything in life that is worth while, it will be due wholly to the Tuskegee Institute, to its officers and teachers. No true graduate of Tuskegee ever forgets the lessons learned there. I am sure I shall not.

V

THE STORY OF A FARMER

By Frank Reid

I AM glad to be able to give some facts regarding what my brother Dow and I have been able to do since leaving the Tuskegee Institute.

We did not graduate, I am sorry to say, but the lessons given us have not been forgotten. These lessons started us on the way to our present success. I do not use the word "success" boastfully, but because it really states a fact: we have done much more than we ever hoped to do, and have been the means of contributing in some slight measure toward the uplifting of the immediate community about us.

We are located at a place called Dawkins, not more than twelve miles from the Tuskegee Institute, and immediately within its sphere of influence.

Our mother and father were born within a few miles of where we now live. Both of our parents, at the time I write, are living, and are each about

THE STORY OF A FARMER

sixty-five years of age; they were, for twenty-five years each, slaves. Neither can read or write. My brother and I each spent about three years at Tuskegee, and, in addition, he attended school for two years at Talladega College.

I had a very thorough course in carpentry, and my brother worked on the Institute farm. We married two sisters, Susie and Lillie Hendon. Shortly after my marriage my beloved wife Susie died, leaving me with one child. My brother's wife still lives; they have three children.

Until ten years ago we, with our father, were renters, all of us working together. But the Sunday evening talks at Tuskegee by Principal Washington, and his urgent insistence, at all times, that Tuskegee graduates and students should try to own land, led us to desire to improve our condition. We were large renters, however; for twenty-three years our father and his relatives had leased and "worked" a tract of 1,100 acres of land, having leased it for ten years at a time. We still lease this tract, and, in addition, rent an additional 480 acres in the same way, ten years at a time. We subrent tracts of this total of 1,580 acres to thirty tenants, charging one and one-half bales of cotton for each one-horse farm. We pay twenty-three bales for the rent of the 1,580 acres. My brother and I run a sixteen-horse farm, doing much of the work ourselves and paying wages to those who work for us. A number of others also work for us on "halves" —that is, we provide the land, furnish the seeds, tools, mules, feed the mules, and equally divide whatever is raised. This is largely done in all the country districts of the South.

About ten years ago we bought in our own right our first land, 320 acres. Since that time we have acquired by purchase another tract containing 285 acres. The first tract we paid for in two years; the other is also paid for. The total of 605 acres, I am glad to say, is without incumbrance of any kind.

The following statements may give some idea as to what we have been able to do since leaving Tuskegee:

During the year 1904 alone, we paid out $5,000, covering debts on land, fertilizers, and money borrowed with which to carry our thirty tenants.

We own sixteen mules and horses, fourteen head of cattle, thirty hogs, and have absolutely no indebtedness of any character.

My brother Dow lives in a good three-room house. My father and I live in a good six-room

A SILO ON THE FARM.

Students filling it with fodder corn. steam-power being used.

THE STORY OF A FARMER

house, with a large, airy hall, and kitchen; it cost us to build, $1,500.

We conduct a large general store, with everything carried in a country store of this kind. The colored Odd Fellows use the hall above our store for their meetings.

The Government post-office is located in our store, and here all of the surrounding community come for their mail.

Our store does a large yearly business averaging about $5,000.

We have a steam-gin and grist-mill. We gin about 500 bales of cotton a season for ourselves and others living near; of the 150 bales got from the land owned and rented by us, 100 are ours, the other 50 belong to our tenants.

We raise large quantities of corn, potatoes, and peas, in addition to our cotton crop.

We are now trying to purchase the 480 acres we have been so long renting.

The church and the schoolhouse are on four acres of land immediately adjoining ours. The church is roomy, well-seated, ceiled and painted, in striking contrast with most of those in the country districts of the South. The schoolhouse has two rooms, and is but partially ceiled, though it is nicely weather-boarded. The school is regularly conducted for five months each year, and part of the time has two teachers. Mr. J. C. Calloway, a Tuskegee graduate, Class of '96, is principal of the school. We are cooperating with Mr. Calloway in an effort to supplement the school funds and secure an additional two months. We helped pay for the land, and gave a part of the money toward the schoolhouse, and have done all possible to help, keeping in mind Principal Washington's oft-repeated statement that "it is upon the country public schools that the masses of the race are dependent for an education."

My brother and I, with our father, it will be noted, own and rent 2,185 acres of land, but we try to help our tenants in every possible way, and, when they desire it, subrent to them such tracts as they desire for ten years, or less. We have established a blacksmith-shop on our land, and do all our own work and most of that of the whole community. Rev. Robert C. Bedford, secretary of the board of trustees, Tuskegee Institute, some time ago visited us, as he does most of the Tuskegee graduates and former students. He is apprised of the correctness of the statements set forth above. He wrote the following much-appreciated compliment to a

THE STORY OF A FARMER

friend regarding our homes and ourselves: "The homes of the Reid brothers are very nicely furnished throughout. Everything is well kept and very orderly. The bedspreads are strikingly white, and the rooms—though I called when not expected—were in the very best of order."

This further statement may not be amiss: Under the guidance of the Tuskegee influences, the annual Tuskegee Negro Conferences, the visits of Tuskegee teachers, etc., the importance of land-buying was early brought to our attention, but because of the crude and inexperienced laborers about us, we found that we could, with advantage to all, rent large tracts of land, subrent to others, and in this way pay no rent ourselves, as these sub-renters did that for us. We could in this way also escape paying taxes, insurance, and other expenses that naturally follow. We could, as many white farmers do, hire wage hands at from $7.50 to $10 a month, with " rations," or arrange to have them work on " halves," as I have already described.

But at last we yielded to the constant pounding received at Tuskegee whenever we would go over, that we ought to own land for ourselves; and then, too, it occurred to me that we might not always have the same whole-souled man to deal with, and that terms might be made much harder. My brother and father agreed, and we set about to purchase the first 320 acres. As I feared, rental values have increased; formerly we rented the 1,100 acres for three bales of cotton; now we give sixteen bales for the same land.

My brother, our father, and I have worked together from the beginning. We have had no disputes or differences; we have worked on the basis of a common property interest.

We have encouraged the people of our community as much as possible to secure homes, buy lands, live decently, and be somebody. The following are some typical examples of thrift and industry in the community about us:

Turner Moore owns 210 acres of land adjoining ours. He was born near where he lives and was over twenty-five years a slave. He has 11 mules and horses and raised 65 bales of cotton last year. His property is all paid for. His brother, Moses Moore, also has 65 acres, all paid for, and Reuben Moore, a nephew, owns 212 acres, all paid for. Their farms join.

James Whitlow, father-in-law of Mr. J. C. Calloway, the teacher referred to, owns 1,137 acres

THE STORY OF A FARMER

in one body, only about two miles from our place. It is all paid for, and the deeds are all recorded at the Macon County Courthouse. He was born right where he now lives, and was twelve years old when freed.

Mr. Whitlow rents a gin, but will own one of his own this year. He also carries on a store. He has 20 tenants, who will raise over 100 bales of cotton this year together. He has raised over 30 himself. He has 20 mules, 3 horses, 30 head of cattle, and about 75 hogs. He does not owe a nickel. His taxes are $60 per year. He has a very good four-room house, besides a kitchen.

Mr. Whitlow has fourteen children, ten boys and four girls, who go to school on our place. He himself can not read or write, but he helps the school and church.

J. C. Calloway was born near us. He graduated from Tuskegee, and has continued to work near his old home. He married James Whitlow's daughter. He has a very good two-room frame house. Mr. Whitlow gave them 40 acres of land, and he is trying to buy an additional 100 acres. He raised 17 bales of cotton this year and 150 bushels of corn. He has 4 horses and mules and 7 head of cattle, besides hogs, chickens, etc. He is very highly thought of in his school work, and is successful as a farmer.

I believe we are doing well. Our community is rated high, and I shall never fail to praise Tuskegee for starting us in the way we are going.

VI

THE STORY OF A CARPENTER

By Gabriel B. Miller

The plantation on which I was born in 1875 is located near Pleasant Hill, Ga. At that time Pleasant Hill was twenty miles from any railroad, and I did not see a railroad train till I was twelve years of age.

I lived on a plantation on which more than two hundred men and women worked for the owner. The children had no especial educational opportunities. Few of them were even permitted to attend the makeshift public school located near. For six months only, of the twelve years my father lived on that plantation, did I attend any school, and that a small one taught by a Southern white woman who had owned my father. When I was twelve years of age my father moved from the plantation on which he had been working "on shares" and rented land which he and his family cultivated. Soon there were thirteen children in his family, of which number I was the second.

TUSKEGEE AND ITS PEOPLE

In December, 1892, I drove a wagon with two bales of cotton to a little Georgia town. While waiting for the wagon preceding me to move off the scales on which the cotton was weighed, I heard a colored man, who had heard of Tuskegee Institute, telling of its advantages, and he quite glowingly recounted the glories of the place as they had been related to him. As he proceeded he informed those gathered about him that at this school a boy could work his way if perchance he could reach the institution. I got nearer to him and heard and treasured every word he said. Especially did I remember his statement that he had been informed that some of the boys graduating from there had not paid a single cent in cash for their education, having worked it all out.

When I reached home that night I told my father of what I had heard. For three successive years our crops had failed and my father was more than $500 in debt. The prospect of interesting him in any project that meant the expenditure of money was discouraging, but an eager desire to secure an education led me to make him a proposition, viz.: that he should permit me during the next year, 1893, to have full and complete charge of the farm, and if I succeeded in settling all of

THE STORY OF A CARPENTER

his indebtedness I was to be released to attend school at Tuskegee, provided I could secure admittance, whether he cleared any money or not. This proposition my father readily agreed to. He sympathized with my ambitions, but the heavy burden of carrying a large family with short-crop returns dwarfed whatever good intentions he might have.

On the first of January, 1893, those of the family who could work joined me in starting early and working late during the whole of the year. We ran a two-horse farm. From that year's work we gathered 25 bales of cotton, 800 bushels of corn, 300 bushels of cow-peas, 250 gallons of sugar-cane sirup, 5 wagon-loads of pumpkins, a great amount of hay and fodder, and picked at night for neighbors about us, white and black, 25 bales of cotton. We had rented two mules and the wagon used that year, but now at the close bought two younger, stronger mules and a new wagon and paid cash for the whole outfit. We settled our indebtedness with everybody, and my father, who had earnestly worked under my supervision along with the others, was very, very happy. Of course, we had a very small balance left—not enough to be of any service to me in keeping me in school except I should be allowed to help myself by working. After " laying the crops by " I made home-made baskets during the summer and sold them, realizing about $16. In one year I had accomplished a task my father thought impossible of accomplishment. He religiously kept his word, and was as enthusiastic about my getting off to school as I was.

I had now learned more of the Tuskegee Institute, and was impatient to reach there. Others, too, became eager and enthusiastic, and so when I started, January 19, 1894, it was a red-letter event in our little community. I left home with only the $16 I had saved from the sale of my baskets. The next morning after reaching Tuskegee I was piloted to the Principal's office and my recommendations requested. I was puzzled. I did not know what was wanted. I had not followed the usual routine and written for permission to enter as students are required to do, but had gone ahead, thinking the presentation of myself all that would be necessary. I had no recommendations, but mustered courage enough to ask for a trial before being refused. My request was granted, and I became a student—proud event in my life!—of the famous Tuskegee Normal and Industrial Institute.

I had always wanted to be a carpenter; as long ago as I can remember this was my ambition, but

THE STORY OF A CARPENTER

when carried to the office of the director of industries he refused to assign me to work there, as that division was filled, but assigned me instead to the sawmilling division. I was not angry, of course. I was too glad to be at Tuskegee; but I was bitterly disappointed, especially after I had seen the carpenter shop, some of the work of the young men, and the imposing buildings on which they had been and were working. I was promised the first vacancy, and that temporarily eased my sorrow. A vacancy did not occur for one and a half years. In the meantime I had become reconciled, and had worked as earnestly as I could to please the instructor in sawmilling. I tried to learn all there was to learn in that division, and at the end of that period could adjust and run proficiently every machine in the sawmilling division. The school cut then, as it does now, most of the lumber used in the carpentry division, and efficient students were needed and desired. My instructor was so well pleased with my progress that he recommended, over my protest, to the director of industries, my retention in the division.

I had kept so busily after the director during those eighteen months to allow me to enter the shop that he could not well refuse to grant my request when a vacancy occurred. I was admitted to the carpenter shop.

For five years I was an apprentice, doing work of every kind. I also took mechanical drawing along with carpentry. When I graduated in 1900 I received not only a diploma from the academic department, but a certificate from the carpentry division as well. I had improved every opportunity, and had a fair knowledge of architectural as well as of mechanical drawing. This latter instruction I had made a place for along with my other studies.

Maj. J. B. Ramsey, the Commandant, had been so well pleased with my general deportment that for years I was commissioned by him to command, as captain, one of the companies of the Tuskegee Institute battalion of cadets. This had pleased and encouraged me very much indeed.

To my surprise, three months before my graduation I was asked to remain in the employ of the Tuskegee Institute as one of the assistant teachers in the carpentry division. I had contracted, however, to do some work at Montgomery, Ala., and I could not accept the place offered. I spent about four months working at my trade in Montgomery, and was again reminded of the offer made me at

THE STORY OF A CARPENTER

Tuskegee. I returned to Tuskegee, but did not remain long, as the Executive Council of the Institute recommended me, when application was made for a competent man to take charge of the carpentry division of the Fort Valley High and Industrial School, Fort Valley, Ga. The terms offered were satisfactory and I accepted the position.

I began work here November 9, 1900, in a shop 30 feet by 60 feet. No tools and no workbenches were provided, only a lot of inexperienced boys to whom I was expected to teach carpentry. I owned a chest of tools, and these I used until the school could secure some. I proceeded at once to make work benches, and my boys had their first lessons in carpentry in providing these. Quite often visitors who come to see us ask if these benches were not made at some factory, they are so well made. We next proceeded to fit out a drawing-room, as I intended that my boys should work—as I had been compelled to do from the very beginning at Tuskegee—from drawings. Everything I had done there had to be carefully worked out in advance, and, knowing the value of that kind of thing, I did not want these boys to have anything less than the kind of instruction I had had. We made tables and desks for the drawing-room; next we ceiled and finished twelve rooms in the main school building that had long been left unfinished. All of the work pleased the authorities of the school, I have reason to know. Near the close of my first term at Fort Valley it was decided to erect a dormitory building for girls. I was asked to submit plans and specifications. My training as a carpenter at Tuskegee had fitted me for just that kind of thing, and I set about designing a building that would meet the requirements of the young women attending Fort Valley.

My plans were finally accepted, and I thought to go on with the erection of the building during the summer, as had been planned; but one or two of the building committee began to object, urging that I was too young, that I had not had enough experience, and that a building of that quality should be erected by a builder of proved reputation. After much delay I was permitted to proceed. I began with ten " green " boys, and they, under my direction as I worked side by side with them, did all of the work except the hanging of the window-sashes, doors, etc. I had outside help in doing this part of the finishing. The building is a real pride to all of us here. It is 36 feet by 78

THE STORY OF A CARPENTER

feet, 2½ stories high, has 22 sleeping-rooms, a splendidly arranged dining-room, 36 feet by 36 feet, and cost $3,200. No one, hereabouts at least, now doubts that I can build anything I say I can. I am glad that so soon after beginning the work here I was able to prove the claims of my Tuskegee instructors as to my fitness for the position for which they had recommended me.

Unfortunately, before I had completed the dormitory for girls, a fire destroyed our main school building with the contents. This fire left us without class-rooms. We took refuge in the Carpenter Shop, and held classes there until money was secured with which to build a training-school for the lower grades. This latter building I also put up entirely with student labor. It contains three large rooms, each 25 feet by 30 feet. The appointments in every way accord with approved hygienic laws. Dr. Wallace Buttrick, Executive Secretary of the General Education Board, spoke complimentarily of the building when he saw it, as one of the few in the State he had seen that met all the requirements of a class-room. We were able to build it for $1,600.

Even during the construction of the training-school I was drawing the plans for a large brick building to replace the one burned. My plans were submitted to friends of the work in the North, and by the time we had finished the training-school we had money enough to begin the brickwork on the new building. By April, 1903, the brickwork was complete, and as we had no additional money we were compelled to allow the building to stand until June, 1904, at which time we were able to resume.

My boys did all of the woodwork, did the hod-carrying, and most of the unskilled labor. The building cost $8,000, and is 86 feet 8 inches by 52 feet 8 inches in its dimensions, is $2\frac{1}{2}$ stories high, and has a deckle roof with dormer windows. The chapel is on the first floor, 6 recitation-rooms on the second floor, and 13 sleeping-rooms for boys on the one-half third-story floor. A basement for storage purposes, 25 feet by 50 feet, is a great convenience.

Of the many contractors and builders who have visited our school-grounds none have failed to speak in praise of the design, the workmanship, the strength, and the relative relation to each other of the school buildings with regard to future additions.

I need not add that this has been very pleasing

THE STORY OF A CARPENTER

to me. I was married December 9, 1904, at Atlanta, Ga., to Miss Mary E. Hobbs.

To me Tuskegee has been all in all, and I still remember with gratitude the man who, in my hearing, spoke so glowingly of the school as I weighed my cotton in the little Georgia town away back in December, 1892.

VII

COTTON-GROWING IN AFRICA

By John W. Robinson

As all autobiographical sketches begin, so do I begin this one. I was born in Bennettsville, S. C., in 1873. Neither of my parents could write their names; but my father could read a little, and taught me the alphabet.

My paternal grandfather was a slave of some intelligence. He was a competent carpenter, had charge of his master's saw- and grist-mills, and kept the accounts of the two mills. His master, who was a member of the State Legislature, was very kind to him. He allowed him a portion of the savings from these industries he was controlling, and even promised him his freedom. The latter he delayed so long that my grandfather ran away. He succeeded in reaching Charleston, S. C. He had secured a ticket and was about to take passage for Canada, when he was captured and returned to his master's home. His master was attending the General Assembly of the State of South Carolina, and it became the overseer's duty to punish the returned fugitive. My grandfather never recovered from the effects of the brutal punishment meted out to him for daring to desire freedom in his own right.

My father was the oldest boy and the second child in a family of five. He was a farmer and a cobbler. At the age of twenty-seven he was married to my mother.

I suppose the history of my mother's life would be monotonous and dull to many ears, but I remember that I never grew tired of hearing her relate its somber happenings. She often told us how her grandmother could relate the thrilling story of her capture on African soil and of being brought to America, of the horrors of the passage, and of much else that I shall always remember.

After their marriage my parents began farming in Bennettsville, Marlborough County, S. C., the place where I was born. I remember most vividly that two-roomed log cabin where my parents' ten children were born—

> "Low and little, and black and old,
> With children as many as it could hold."

However, my father soon began working for wages, and received $10 per month and the proverbial "rations"—three pounds of meat and a peck of meal per week. What a financier he must have been, for from that mean sum he managed to save $50 or $75 each year, and I still cherish the memory of how fondly I felt those crisp greenbacks once a year. He brought them home every Christmas and allowed each member of the family to feel them—yes, even caress them.

When I was about nine years of age I entered the public school of the community, which was in session about four months in a year, opening late in the fall and going through the winter. My parents were so delighted and gratified at the progress I made that I was occasionally privileged to spend one month in the subscription school conducted near by during the summer.

When I was fourteen years of age a great sorrow visited our home. My mother died. I often wonder if any one can realize what it means to lose a mother without having suffered that bereavement. My father did not marry again.

About this time the authorities opened a school nearer us than the one I had been attending, but the teachers were usually very incompetent and my progress was seriously hindered.

The absorbing desire of my life had been to

COTTON-GROWING IN AFRICA

some day graduate from some institution of learning, but I found myself at eighteen years of age far from the goal of my ambition. I became alarmed. I realized what it would mean to grow to manhood in ignorance; I also knew that there were seven children younger than I to be cared for. I seriously thought the matter over. I finally broached it to my father, and he consented that I should try to make a way for myself.

I rented a small farm, trusting that by cultivating it I would be able to clear enough money to begin my education. I began wrong, for I had in advance mortgaged my crop. I began with $75, but when the year closed I had only $10. However, my aspirations were not to be daunted; I was resolved on going to school.

With this $10 I purchased the necessary books, paid my entrance fee, and entered the village graded school. I was poorly clad, and much of the time was without food, but I felt that I could not even ask my father for assistance because of his responsibility in caring for the younger children. I was constant, however, in my endeavor to find work, and finally a companion and I succeeded in getting an old farmhouse about three miles from the village in which to live. In a measure this suited me, for I loved the country.

The house was an old, dilapidated one, and I do not see now how we stood that first severe winter; but though I was in rags and my food was often roasted potatoes or peas with a little salt, I did not miss a single day's schooling that year, and great was my joy and satisfaction when, at the end of the year, I stood at the head of my class.

During this time I had done such work in the surrounding neighborhood as could be obtained. My Saturdays and afternoons were spent in splitting rails, chopping wood, driving garden palings, and doing any other work that would enable me to exist. Although I had stinted myself and had often gone without food, at the end of the year I was $12 in debt. But this was not sufficient to make me despair.

When vacation came I immediately sought work, and though I was diligent in my application to it when I had obtained it, steady employment was not to be had. My wages were never more than fifty cents a day, but I often received less. For two years I lived in this way. At the expiration of that time I decided that it would benefit me to enter a higher institution of learning. I

COTTON-GROWING IN AFRICA

knew that this would mean that I must have more remunerative employment.

By some means my attention was directed to the orange industry of Florida, and in the summer of 1894 I regretfully left my companions and relatives, went to Deland, Fla., and secured the desired work. The winter proved to be an unusually cold one, and the orange industry was greatly hindered; therefore I was soon out of employment, and at the season of the year when I most needed it. I was not long idle, however, for the very cause of my loss of work opened another avenue; I was kept busy chopping wood. Though I went to Florida penniless, at the end of six months I had saved $60.

It was at Deland that I learned of the magnificent opportunities afforded earnest young men and women at Tuskegee Institute. I at once made application to become a student. That morning I did not know that such a school existed; that night, while I slept, the Southern Railway was bearing my letter of application to Mr. Washington. My anxiety almost reached fever-heat during those few intervening days that I waited for an answer, and my joy was boundless when it came, setting forth the requirements for admittance. I sent a portion of the money I had saved to my father. With the rest I bought some necessary clothing, and left Deland far behind for Tuskegee.

I shall always remember how little and insignificant I felt when I entered the school-grounds and was told that all those buildings and all those acres of ground were a part of the Tuskegee Institute. I had read of it in the circular of information which was sent me when I applied for admission, but the realization was, to me, almost overpowering. After paying my entrance fee and purchasing my school-books I had $15 left. Thus I began what has proved to be a " new life."

Fifteen dollars were, of course, an inadequate sum with which to pay my expenses through the day-school, and so I was permitted to enter the night-school, as so many others as poor as I had done. This means that I was given an opportunity to work at some industry during the day and attend classes at night. I was not only receiving training at an industry, being provided with food, shelter, and fuel, and receiving instruction at night, but I was earning enough over my board to be placed to my credit in the school's treasury to help pay my board when I should enter the day-school.

My first term was spent at work on Marshall

COTTON-GROWING IN AFRICA

Farm, where the greater part of the school's farming was at that time done.

When I entered Tuskegee I had no thought of preparing myself for returning to farm life. Even the word "farm" brought to my mind visions of dull, hard work and drudgery without comforts. I had not been at the Tuskegee Institute long, however, before I was led to know that "agriculture" is the very highest of all industrial callings. I had never known that agriculture had so many subdivisions, that soils could be analyzed and treated, that rotation of crops enriched the soil, that a certain crop planted season after season on the same soil made it poor, because it was ridding it of some life-giving chemical. To me soils simply "wore out." But through lectures and practical experiments my agricultural horizon began to expand, and a sense of the beauty of the industry grew upon me.

It was to me a marvelous thing to go into the dairy and take milk but recently milked, pour it into the Sharpless Separator, set the machine in motion, and behold a stream of rich, sweet cream flow from one avenue of escape, while a foamy jet of milk passed from another. There, too, I learned cheese-making and butter-making.

TUSKEGEE AND ITS PEOPLE

My school life was filled with difficulties because of financial embarrassments. I was one of the competitors in the first Trinity Church (Boston) Prize Contest, founded at the school by Dr. E. Winchester Donald, successor of Phillips Brooks, and rector of Trinity until his death, and I remember that I was greatly discomfited because the socks I wore had no feet in them, and my shoes had that afternoon been sewed with thread blackened with soot.

However, I was the successful contestant, the first winner of the prize of $25. The next day I provided myself with new shoes and socks. I also received my diploma that same year, 1897, within two days of receiving the prize, and was very happy to receive it and the diploma at the same time.

Two summers and one winter after graduating I taught school at Mamie, Ala. When I was not teaching I worked on the farm of the family with which I boarded. For this work I received very little pay, but I had been taught at Tuskegee that it was better to work for nothing than to be idle—a Booker T. Washington precept.

The second winter I was first assistant in the Ozark city school, Ozark, Ala., and was offered

COTTON-GROWING IN AFRICA

the principalship for the next term, but I declined in order to further pursue postgraduate studies in agriculture at Tuskegee. I remained there for six months. I then went West, to Rockford, Ill., to do practical work in that section for the purpose of strengthening and improving the theory and practise already learned.

It was harvesting season and I soon secured work. I put all my energy into the work of the rugged Western farm and succeeded admirably in following the threshing-machine, in husking corn, and in doing the other farm labors common to Western fall and winter seasons. My first four months were spent on the farm of a widow. After the harvesting was over she offered me the farm, with its implements, barns, horses, and dairy herd, if I would remain and pay her certain percentages of the profits, but I told her that I was only a student in search of knowledge.

The next spring I secured work with a very progressive Irishman. He was a farmer, as well as secretary and treasurer of a modern creamery and butter factory. This work I preferred, because it was along my chosen line, and of a very high grade.

For one year I worked in this establishment,

and was not absent from duty even one day. My employer once said to me that he had heard and also read that Negroes were lazy, shiftless, and untrustworthy. He had not come into contact with enough Negroes to draw his own conclusions, so he asked me if there were more like me. I told him that I did not consider myself an exception, but that I had had the advantages of superior training at Tuskegee. He did not know before that I was a Tuskegee graduate. He seemed surprised to know that a graduate would work as a common farm-hand. He said he had found no white ones who would. I then explained to him that I was seeking a comprehensive knowledge of farming conditions North and South. I value that year on those Western farms next to my training at Tuskegee.

I was planning to return to the South and start a farm of my own, when I was asked by Mr. Washington to join a company of Tuskegee young men who were wanted to go to Africa for the purpose of experimenting in cotton-growing under the German Government. It was a call I could not resist. Here was a chance for the largest possible usefulness. Here I could have a part in a monumental undertaking, and I gladly agreed to go.

COTTON-GROWING IN AFRICA

The wages offered were flattering, and all expenses in connection with the trip were borne by the Kolonial Komittee of the German Government. The Executive Council of the Institute selected Shepherd L. Harris, Allen L. Burks, and myself, all graduates of the school, and Mr. James N. Calloway, a member of the Faculty, who had had charge of the school's largest farm, and who was selected to head the expedition. We sailed from New York on November 3, 1900, and reached Togo by way of Hamburg on December 31, 1900. Later five additional Tuskegee students joined us, but of the original party I am the only one left. A report of the beginnings of our work was published after two years, with elaborate illustrations to commemorate what we had been able to accomplish. Samples of the cotton made into hose and various other articles were distributed among those interested in the success of the experiment. That report may be secured from the Kolonial-Wirtschaftliches Komittee, Berlin, Germany.

Not long since I sent to Principal Washington a summary of the work we have been trying to do. He regularly insists that Tuskegee graduates shall send him reports of what they are doing, and my letter to him was in response to that request. We keep in touch with Tuskegee and its work after leaving the institution through a correspondence prized by every graduate of the school. The summary I include here, as it may be of interest to the reader:

At the outset it was very difficult to excite any interest at all in our work on the part of the natives. For some reason they mistrust every proposition made them by a foreigner, and in the beginning they would not even accept the gift of cotton-seeds from us. They claimed that if they should accept our seeds we would come again and claim our own with usury. Many of the Europeans here said that the natives would never become interested in the movement. But we worked on, and now already in the farming districts are hundreds of native cotton farms. Now they no longer mistrust us, but they come and ask for cotton-seeds, and a conservative estimate places the incoming native harvest near the thousand-bale mark. Of course the native methods are very irrational. They cultivate their cotton altogether as a secondary crop. But we are content, at the beginning, to let them cultivate in their own way.

We find distributed through the colony not less than three distinct species of cotton, with some hybrids and varieties; but none of these are indigenous, and, having been left in a neglected state

COTTON-GROWING IN AFRICA

for centuries, are consequently not far removed from nature and are not so remunerative when put under even the best culture. The seeds imported from America are not able to survive the greatly changed conditions of climate. Here is our greatest obstacle. Our course was plain. If we did not have a plant that exactly suited us, we had to make it.

The production of a commercial plant is very important. Our present domestic seeds will yield about four hundred pounds of seed-cotton per acre, and the character of the fruit and the arrangement upon the stalk make it very expensive to harvest. Besides, the stalk grows too much to a tree and is not prolific proportionately, and the quality of the lint is equal to American "middling." We are trying to develop a plant that will yield 1,000 pounds of seed-cotton to the acre, with a lint equal in quality to fully good "middling" or to Allen's $1\tfrac{7}{8}$-inch staple.

Now suppose we succeed in making this plant as I have above outlined; the 4,000 acres under cultivation would then at least produce 2,000 bales of seed-cotton where they now produce but 1,000 bales. We can see how greatly the annual income of the natives will be increased. Such a plant is forthcoming.

Through selection and crossing of American and native cottons we have obtained a new variety, which is satisfactory in every primary respect. It is more hardy than the average American plant and fifty per cent more productive than the average native plant. A sample of the lint of this new, would-be variety was submitted to the Chamber of Commerce in Berlin, and it was pronounced good in every way, and brought in January, 1904, about twenty cents a pound.

There is one feature that I would like to speak about before I have done with the subject, because I know it will please you. In one of the letters you wrote me some time ago you advised me to "labor earnestly, quietly, and soberly, discharging my duty in the way that would eventually make me one of the most influential persons in the community." Being faithful in small things is one of the fundamental principles of Tuskegee, and is what I am able to do without even striving. It has become natural for me to be faithful, it matters not how small or insignificant the service. I find myself to-day possessing much influence in the work in which I am now engaged.

In order to make secure the work begun and to insure a normal and well-balanced progress for the future, it was recommended to institute, along with the present undertaking, what I am pleased to call "A Cotton-School and Plant-Breeding Station." At this school are gathered young men from all over the colony, who come for a two-years' course in modern methods of farming. The boys are to be taught some of the simple rules

COTTON-GROWING IN AFRICA

and practises of agriculture. The boys are 45 in number, representing the most intelligent classes; the station consists of 250 acres of land, 8 oxen, 2 asses, 1 horse, farm implements, cotton-gin, press, etc. Such an institution appeared to me necessary to the healthy progress of the undertaking. There will soon be in operation 3 ginning- and pressing-stations run by steam-power, besides a dozen or more hand-gins. This, I believe, tells the whole story. My health is very good. I hope you will write me often, because your letters are always so interesting and helpful.

That my life has been as useful and successful as it has is due to the training and inspiration received at Tuskegee Institute, perhaps not so much to the agricultural department, for I did not finish that course, but to the general awakening and stimulating influence which permeates and is a part of the training of Tuskegee students.

And now while I write, and daily as I work, I am prompted on to better and stronger efforts because of the Tuskegee in embryo that looms before me. And as I think, and work, and write, I am gratified because of the assurance that I am only one of that increasing host whose loyal hearts and useful lives shall make Tuskegee live forever.

VIII

THE STORY OF A TEACHER OF COOKING

By Mary L. Dotson

I GRADUATED with the Class of 1900, Tuskegee Institute. It was the culmination of an event to which my mother and I had long looked forward.

I was born in 1879, in a small country village in the southwestern part of Alabama. My mother was the exceptional colored woman of our community. She was a dressmaker and tailoress and had all the work she could do. She owned her own home, a quite comfortable one, and earned continuously from her work a tidy sum of money.

I have always counted myself fortunate to have had such a home and such a mother. Very few of the colored people about us owned their own homes; the village school was a poor makeshift, and it was in session only two to four months in a year—that is, when some one could be secured to teach it for the very small salary paid. Both my father and mother had great respect for educa-

A TEACHER OF COOKING

tionally equipped people, and desired that their children should have the opportunity to secure educational advantages. They tried in every possible way to interest the people in their own welfare, at least to the extent of supplementing the meager public-school fund, so as to provide decent educational facilities for the children. This effort failed. My mother had a room added to her home, and in it conducted, with my sister's help, a school for the children of the community. Two of my sisters had been sent away to school, one to Selma and the other to Talladega. In addition to the school conducted at our home, my mother was able to get the cooperation of some of the people in other parts of the county, and two other schools were started. These schools were afterward taken up, and have since become helpful factors in the life of the people.

My first lessons were given in the home, and my mother always claimed that I learned quite rapidly. As soon as I was old enough she also made me take lessons in sewing. Sewing made no appeal to me, however, but cooking did, and whenever possible I would steal away to my grandmother's to cook with her. Most of the time I was only permitted to wash dishes, but after a while

TUSKEGEE AND ITS PEOPLE

I was permitted to help with her cooking. Soon I was able to make cakes for my father's store. He was always very proud that his " little " daughter was able to replenish his stock when it was exhausted.

At eight years of age I was sent to Meridian, Miss., to stay with an older sister and attend school. The advantages there were far superior to those provided for me at my home. After remaining two years at Meridian I went to Memphis, again in search of better school facilities. I have said that even at my age I had a fondness for cooking. At Memphis I had my first cooking lesson, this lesson being given along with the eighth grade work of the public school. I was delighted, but my aunt refused to allow me to practise in the home, however, and so all the practise I got was at school.

While in Memphis, a Tuskegee Institute graduate came there to teach in the colored public schools. Though we had lived in Alabama, we had not, until that time, heard of the Tuskegee Institute. The loyalty of that graduate to the school, the stories of the opportunities provided, and all, delighted my mother, my aunt, and myself, and it was decided that I should be sent there.

A TEACHER OF COOKING

I entered the Tuskegee Institute in December, 1894, and was assigned, after examination, to the Junior class, the first class of the normal department. I remained at Tuskegee during the following summer and worked in the students' dining-room as a waitress. The next year I was compelled to enter the night-school so as to help lighten my mother's burden. I knew nothing of the science of foods; nothing at all, at that time, of anything that indicated that cooking is a real science. None but girls of the Senior class were then permitted to take cooking lessons, but I was often able to provide some excuse for visiting the very small and incompletely furnished room used for that purpose. I picked up much useful information in that way.

When I reached the A Middle class, next to the Senior class, the young women of that class were permitted to take cooking lessons.

Now I was to learn cooking. I had long desired the opportunity, and the chance had come at last. The study of foods was among the first lessons brought to my attention. While anxious to know all that was to be taught, I could never see the reasons for knowing. I wanted to cook food, and that, with me, was the end.

TUSKEGEE AND ITS PEOPLE

I began to study chemistry in the academic department, and when it was applied in my cooking lessons my eyes were opened. I now saw much that I had not dreamed of. A cooking teacher, a noted expert from Wisconsin, came to the school about that time and lectured not only to the cooking classes, but to the young women teachers, and to the married women of the Institute families. I was especially detailed to work with her, and was put to working out a diet for the students' boarding department. This instruction, with that of my regular instructor, convinced me that here was a real profession. I continued until the end of my school days to carry, along with all of my academic work, progressive work in cooking.

I had made such progress that when I came to graduate, Mrs. Washington, who is in charge of the industries for girls, offered me a vacancy in the cooking division. I did not feel that I was adequate to the requirements of the place, and so remarked to Mrs. Washington and my instructor. They recommended that I spend the summer at the Chautauqua Summer School, New York. I prepared to go immediately following the Tuskegee commencement exercises. A scholarship was

A TEACHER OF COOKING

secured for me. Domestic science teachers of proved efficiency are in charge there. They were pleased with what I had already been able to accomplish. My work was with the classes taking courses in chemistry, physiology, bacteriology, management of classes, and cooking demonstration.

At the end of the summer I felt stronger than ever, and returned to Tuskegee in the fall with real enthusiasm. I first began my work in the little room in which I had been taught. Another academic class of girls had now been admitted to the cooking classes, the three upper ones.

When Dorothy Hall, the building in which all of the industries for girls are located, was completed, my division was given a suite of rooms, an assistant was provided, and the work broadened and made more useful than ever. Under this division we now have a model kitchen, a regular kitchen in which the practise-cooking of the girls is done, two dining-rooms, a model bedroom, a model sitting-room, and a bathroom.

Principal Washington has insisted from year to year that, since cooking is so fundamental, every young woman, in the day-school at least, shall take lessons in cooking. For the current school year, 1904-'05, 458 young women are receiving instruction.

The course covers, in its entirety, four years, but is so comprehensive that even one and two years fit young women for the cooking of ordinary foods. Each of these girls is required to attend upon the outlined catalogue course of instruction, and in addition, from time to time, upon lectures bearing upon the several subjects comprehended under domestic science. The furnishing of the rooms is simple, but ample; the furniture, in the main, being made by the young women in the upholstering division. It has been widely praised by all who have seen it.

After teaching for two years, I requested leave of absence for one year so as to attend the Domestic-Science School of the Young Women's Christian Association, Boston. This additional study, of course, helped me very much. My studies were of foods, of the home, the teaching of demonstration and settlement classes, etc. Much other useful information also came my way.

When I returned to Tuskegee the next year I felt more able than ever to be of assistance to the girls who come to us. I was better able to outline my course of study. The thing that pleased

A TEACHER OF COOKING

me greatly, however, both at Chautauqua and at Boston, was the fact that my former Tuskegee training was commented on so favorably, as having been planned along properly comprehensive lines.

No part of the Tuskegee Institute work is more valuable than that of the domestic training. It is the policy of the institution to give special attention to the training of girls in all that pertains to dress, health, physical culture, and general housekeeping.

The girls are constantly under the strict and watchful care of the dean of the woman's department, Miss Jane E. Clark, a graduate of Oberlin College, a woman of liberal attainments and culture, and an example to them in all that makes for the development of character; of Mrs. Booker T. Washington, the director of industries for girls, and of the women teachers, a body in every way representative of the qualities the girls are besought to seek to attain. A corps of matrons, four in number, specially assist the dean of the woman's department and keep in close individual touch with the girls.

My own connection with the girls is in the cooking classes, as I have indicated, and in the Parker Model Home and the Practise Cottage. The

Parker Model Home is the home of the young women who each year reach the Senior class. Eight large, conveniently arranged rooms are set apart for them, and they are taught things by having to do them. The class, as a whole, is required to do actual work in the line of general housekeeping, cooking and serving food, and laundering.

In order to give practical demonstration in housekeeping and to develop the sense of responsibility in the work, a four-room house has been set aside, in which the Senior girls "keep house." Four girls at a time live in this house and have the entire care of it. They do all the work that pertains to ordinary housekeeping, from the Monday morning's washing to the Saturday's preparation for Sunday. They are also charged with the responsibility of purchasing the food supplies which they consume. Three dollars are allowed as the weekly expenditure for food. In view of the low prices that obtain for provisions here, four girls can live comfortably on this small allowance and have variety and plenty, and at the same time very wholesome food. Thus the lesson of economy is taught in the most effective way. The girls learn to appreciate the purchasing power of money,

A MODEL DINING-ROOM.

From the department where table-service is taught.

A TEACHER OF COOKING

a kind of training which boarding-students, who have so much done for them, do not get. They acquire the habit of evolving their own plans, of exercising unhampered their own tastes. Regularity, system, exactness, neatness, and the feeling of responsibility, are all developed in this way.

In both the Parker Model Home and the Practise Cottage I have charge, with my assistant, of the oversight of what is done in the direction of providing food, cooking it, serving it, etc.

Twenty-one classes a week are now taught; the preparatory classes one hour per week, and the normal classes two to three hours per week. The girls are required to work in groups, to wear white aprons, caps, and sleeves, and to bring to the classes towels and holders. Each girl brings her own blank books and keeps, through the year, a full report of each lesson given.

Most of the girls who come to us know absolutely nothing of cooking and housekeeping. They are, as a rule, like most beginners, more anxious to make cakes, candies, pies, etc., than to make bread, to care for utensils, and learn the practical things most necessary. Improvement soon follows, however.

We do some outside "extension work," in addition to what has been enumerated: a cooking class in the town of Tuskegee for those unable to attend the school at all, and classes for the children at the Children's House, the model training-school of the institution, where they are given understandable lessons in cooking and housekeeping. A bedroom, a dining-room, a bathroom, and a kitchen are also provided in connection with the Children's House.

I am happy in the thought that I have a part in this fundamental, home-building part of the instruction being given the girls who come from thirty-six States and territories of the Union, and from Cuba and Porto Rico and other foreign countries, to attend this famous school, of which I am myself a graduate.

When the girls are fitted to make better homes, a better people are the result. To have some part in this work was a fond wish while a student, and is a prized privilege now that I have the opportunity to render some slight service in return for all that Tuskegee has done for me.

IX

A WOMAN'S WORK

By Cornelia Bowen

Of myself and the work I have done there is not a great deal to say. I was born at Tuskegee, Ala., on a part of the very ground now occupied by the famous Tuskegee Institute. The building first used by the school as an industrial building for girls was the house in which I was born. That old building (and two others, as well) is carefully preserved by the institution as an old landmark, and never do I go to Tuskegee that I do not search it out among the more imposing and pretentious buildings which have come during the later years of the school's history. This building and the two other small ones were on the property when it was acquired by Principal Washington.

My mother lived the greater part of her life at this place as the slave of Colonel William Bowen, who owned the plot of ground upon which the Tuskegee Institute now stands. The birthplace of my mother was Baltimore, Md. She was taught to read by her master's daughter in Baltimore, and was never forbidden to read by those who owned her in Alabama.

When a child, I could never understand why she read so well and could not write. I was very sorry at times that she could read and was not like other children's mothers whom I knew. She always knew when I did not get my lessons, and often the hours of play that were dear to me were taken away until my reading lesson was learned. Sundays, with my sisters gathered about her knees, we would sit for hours listening as mother would read church hymns for us. These days were days of freedom, as I do not remember, and know nothing of, those of slavery. My mother always refrained from telling her children frightful stories of the awful sufferings of the slave days. She occupied the position of seamstress and house-servant in her mistress's home, and was never allowed to mingle with plantation slaves.

My first teacher was a good-hearted Southern white woman, who knew my mother well and lived in the town of Tuskegee.

She taught me to read from McGuffey's First Reader. I often read my lessons by looking at the ctures, for I did not know one word from an-

A WOMAN'S WORK

other—so far as the letters were concerned. She detected one day, however, that I was looking out into the street and at the same time reading what I supposed to be the lesson. From that time on she devoted herself to teaching me so that I should know letters, and that I should read properly. She always claimed that I was an apt pupil. At any rate, at a very early age I was able to both read and write. As I grew older I was sent with my sisters to the public schools of Tuskegee. It was always my ambition, it is not immodest to say, to excel in whatever I undertook. That which brought tears to my eyes quicker than any other one thing was to have some member of my class recite a better lesson, or "turn me down"—that is, go up ahead of me in the class.

Having been brought up in the Methodist Sunday-school, I later joined the Methodist Church. Mr. Lewis Adams, a Trustee of the Tuskegee Institute, was then Superintendent of the Methodist Sunday-school. He was very desirous that the young boys and girls of the Sunday-school should take an active part in the work. I was given a class of girls to teach much older than myself. They tried to disgust me at times by paying no attention to my teaching. I was not to be discouraged, although I cried many times because of their conduct. My own sister, who was a member of the class, also rebelled because I was younger than she; she thought that she should be teaching me instead of having it otherwise. It was the common opinion of the girls that even if I could read better than any of them, they were older and should be shown the preference. I owe much of my interest in the study of the Bible to my mother and to Mr. Lewis Adams, the faithful worker and Sunday-school Superintendent. Mr. Adams was in those early days as he is now, the leader of the colored people of the town of Tuskegee in all that went to make for the uplifting of his people. I can pay no better tribute to him than to quote what Principal Washington himself says in his monumental autobiography, Up from Slavery:

In the midst of the difficulties which I encountered in getting the little school started, and since then through a period of nineteen years, there are two men among all the many friends of the school in Tuskegee upon whom I have depended constantly for advice and guidance; and the success of the undertaking is largely due to these men, from whom I have never sought any-

A WOMAN'S WORK

thing in vain. I mention them simply as types. One is a white man and an ex-slaveholder, Mr. George W. Campbell; the other is a black man and an ex-slave, Mr. Lewis Adams. These were the men who wrote to General Armstrong for a teacher.

Mr. Campbell is a merchant and banker, and had had little experience in dealing with matters pertaining to education. Mr. Adams was a mechanic, and had learned the trades of shoemaking, harness-making, and tinsmithing during the days of slavery. He had never been to school a day in his life, but in some way he had learned to read and write while a slave. From the first, these two men saw clearly what my plan of education was, sympathized with me, and supported me in every effort. In the days which were darkest financially for the school, Mr. Campbell was never appealed to when he was not willing to extend all the aid in his power. I do not know two men—one an ex-slaveholder, one an ex-slave—whose advice and judgment I would feel more like following in everything which concerns the life and development of the school at Tuskegee than those of these two men.

I have always felt that Mr. Adams, in a large degree, derived his unusual powers of mind from the training given his hands in the process of mastering well three trades during the days of slavery.

TUSKEGEE AND ITS PEOPLE

I did not graduate from the public schools as children do nowadays in the cities. Mr. Booker T. Washington's coming to Tuskegee and the establishment of the Tuskegee Normal School put an end to the public-school work on "Zion Hill," where the Tuskegee public school for colored children was located. I was one of the first of the students examined for entrance in the school. Mr. Washington gave the examination in arithmetic, grammar, and history. I never knew what a sentence was, nor that it had a subject and a predicate before he said so. I doubted very seriously the existence of such terms as these new ones mentioned by him. I thought I knew grammar, and I did, so far as I had been taught, but I had no insight into its real meaning and use. Mr. Washington decided after my examination that I would make a good Junior pupil. It was all new to me and I could not understand all of the new words, even though simple they were, used by him. He himself took charge of our classes, and I have always been very proud that I can say that he was my teacher. He was most particular in regard to spelling and the right use of verbs. As a history teacher he was the best I have had the privilege of studying under. I have often said

A WOMAN'S WORK

that if he could teach the classes in the beginning of history and grammar, and give talks on spelling at Tuskegee as he did when I was a pupil there, many who finish at Tuskegee would be thankful in the years to come. However, he can not do this until he is relieved of the great burden of raising funds for the school.

The industrial departments at Tuskegee were not, of course, so elaborate and so many while I was a pupil there. My four years at Tuskegee were given wholly to class-room work. To my class, that graduated in 1885—the first one to graduate, we proudly boast—three Peabody medals were awarded for excellence in scholarship. Our diplomas were also graded. We took an examination for the medals, as there were ten in the graduating class. I was awarded one of the medals. The Class of '85 had high ideals and always regretted that any member should receive a second-grade diploma. I was very thankful to learn after two weeks' waiting that, in the opinion of the Faculty, I was worthy of a first-grade diploma.

After graduating, I was employed as the principal of the training-school—now known as the "Children's House"—of the Tuskegee Institute. Feeling that I could be of more service to my people, and could better teach in the outside world the principles for which Tuskegee stands, I resigned my work at Tuskegee, after several terms, for a broader field of usefulness.

A call reached Mr. Washington in 1888 for a teacher to begin a work in the vicinity of Mt. Meigs, Ala., similar to the work done at Tuskegee, but, of course, on a smaller scale. Mr. E. N. Pierce, of Plainville, Conn., had resolved to do something in the way of providing better school facilities for the colored people living on a large plantation, into the possession of which he had come. Mr. Washington answered the call while in Boston, and telegraphed me that he thought me the proper person to take charge of and carry on the settlement work Mr. Pierce and his friends had in mind.

I found at Mt. Meigs, after studiously investigating conditions, that the outlook for support was far from hopeful. Not one person in the whole community owned a foot of land, and heavy crop mortgages were the burden of every farmer. It became evident at once that pioneer work was very much needed. Homes were neglected, and the sacredness of family life was unknown to most of the people. The prospect was a gloomy one.

A WOMAN'S WORK

The little Baptist church in which the older people gathered for worship two Sundays in each month badly needed repairing.

I began first of all to connect myself with the Sunday-school, and taught there every Sunday. I organized a large class of the older people and encouraged them in every way to attend the Sunday-school every Sunday with the children. None of these mothers or fathers could read or write.

I taught them Scripture verses by repeating verse after verse till they were able to recite them for me. I also sought to teach them to read, and quite a large number can read now because of the opportunities provided by my Sunday-school class. I have kept this class of older people together, and it is one of the most active ones of all. We have studied together many other things aside from the Sunday-school lessons, and it has been necessary to do so, because the people have none of the opportunities provided for those who live in the towns and cities. I was early much encouraged to note that my efforts were appreciated by the people.

I was often called upon to act as arbiter in all kinds of difficult and unpleasant disputes involving family relations and other differences among the people. Many and many a time did I take the place of the minister and speak to the people when he could not be present.

To teach the people self-help, the surest sign of progress, we decided to plan for a main school building which should mark the center of our activities. This building we were able to erect at a cost of $2,000, and it is a satisfaction to the people of the community that they alone paid every cent of the cost, not one penny coming from the outside. The struggle was a long one, a hard one, with bad crops and other hard conditions interfering with our plans.

This building is a two-story one, well ventilated, roomy, and accommodates 300 pupils. From the first we have sought to follow in the footsteps of the parent institution, and have had the industries taught; agriculture was introduced at once.

A large Trades Building was soon erected and teachers from Tuskegee secured to help in the work. Blacksmithing, wheelwrighting, carpentry, painting, and agriculture have been provided for the young men, and cooking, laundering, housekeeping, and sewing for the young women.

The following buildings we now have in addition to those named: a dormitory for girls, a

THE CULTURE OF BEES.
Students at work in the apiary.

A WOMAN'S WORK

blacksmithing-shop, and a teachers' home. More than 4,000 pupils have come under the influence of the school.

I have continuously, for seventeen years, with the exception of a short period, been in charge of the school; during the absence referred to I was studying in New York city, and afterward, through the generosity of a friend, was able to spend one year in Queen Margaret's College, Glasgow, Scotland.

I am pleased with the progress the people have made. Many now own their own homes, and eight and ten persons are no longer content to sleep in one-room log cabins, as was only too true during the earlier years of my work. I have regularly had "mothers' meetings," and these have raised the home life of the people to a higher standard. I know what I am saying when I state that sacred family ties are respected and appreciated as never before in this immediate region.

The emotional church life of the people no longer prevails hereabouts, and the minister preaches forty minutes, instead of two hours as formerly.

Many farmers are out of debt, and a mortgage upon a man's crop is as disreputable as a saloon.

TUSKEGEE AND ITS PEOPLE

The Mt. Meigs Institute is the first school of its kind in Alabama to demonstrate the fact that a school planted among the people in the rural districts of the South will make for intelligent, honest, thrifty citizenship. The success of this work made possible the establishment of many similar schools that have been planted in Alabama and other parts of the South.

Of the young men and women who have attended my school I can not speak too highly. Sixty have graduated, and fifty-seven of the number are still living. Not only they, but many who could not afford to stay and graduate, are at work in an effort to help their less fortunate brethren. Thirty-six of my graduates have taken academic or trade courses in other schools, twenty-one of them at Tuskegee Institute. Ten have graduated from Tuskegee, or from other schools. Thirty-eight of them have learned trades, and all of them are at work and prosperous. They include dressmakers, cooks, housekeepers, laundresses, carpenters, blacksmiths, wheelwrights, painters, etc. Several are successful farmers, and one of the girls is a large cotton-planter and general farmer. Two are successful merchants in Birmingham, Ala.; one is a prominent minister, having also taken a course

A WOMAN'S WORK

at the Virginia Union Seminary, Richmond, Va.; one is in charge of an orphan asylum, and several are teachers; one taught with me for seven years after having also graduated from Tuskegee. Thirty have married, fifteen have bought homes, one has property valued at $7,000, others have property ranging in value from $800 to $2,000. Of the sixty, only four have failed to maintain their moral character.

Six teachers are now employed; we really need another. About 30 boarding pupils are regularly enrolled, with 250 pupils in daily attendance from near-by homes.

The school is conducted just as economically as it well can be; the annual expense is about $2,000, of which sum I have insisted that the people themselves shall annually meet one-half.

If I have been of any service to my people, I owe it all to Mr. Washington and to one of the noblest women that ever lived, Mrs. Booker T. Washington, née Davidson, both of whom indelibly impressed upon me while attending the Tuskegee Institute those lessons which led me to want to spend myself in the helping of my people.

X

UPLIFTING THE SUBMERGED MASSES

By W. J. Edwards

I was born in Snow Hill, Wilcox County, Ala., in the year 1870. My mother died when I was twelve months old. About five or six years after this, perhaps, my father went away from Snow Hill; the next I heard he was dead. Thus at the age of six I was left without father or mother. I was then placed in the care of my old grandmother, who did all that was in her power to send me to the school located near us. Often for weeks I would go to school without anything but bread to eat. Occasionally she could secure a little piece of meat.

I well remember one morning, when I had started to school and she had given me all the meat that we had in the house, how it worried me that she should have nothing left for herself but bread. Worrying over our cramped condition, I resolved that what she did for me should not be thrown away. I longed for the time when I could repay her for all she had done for me.

UPLIFTING THE SUBMERGED

At the age of twelve it pleased the Almighty God to take from me my grandmother, my only dependence. I was now left to fight the battle of life alone. I need not tell of the hard times and sufferings that I experienced until I entered school at the Tuskegee Institute. But knowing that I was without parents, and being sick most of the time, my hardships can be imagined.

Through a minister I heard of the Tuskegee Normal and Industrial Institute in the early part of 1888, and so favorably was it recommended that I decided I would rent two acres of land and raise a crop, and take the proceeds and go to Tuskegee the following fall. After paying my rents and other small debts I had $20 left with which to buy my clothes and start for Tuskegee, which I did, starting on the 27th of December, 1888, and arriving at Tuskegee on the first day of January, 1889, with $10. I had walked most of the way. I was at Tuskegee for four and one-half years. I managed to stay there for that length of time by working one day in the week and every other Saturday during the term and all of the vacations.

During my Senior year I was helped by Mr. R. O. Simpson, the owner of the plantation on which I was reared. I had trouble that year in deciding just what I should do after graduation. It had been my conviction that I must be a lawyer or a minister. In contemplating the idea of becoming a lawyer, however, I could not see wherein I could carry out the Tuskegee Idea of uplifting the masses. The ministerial profession was very little better, since the work of the minister in our section of the country must be limited almost wholly to one denomination. So I finally decided to try to plant an institution similar to the Tuskegee School, an undenominational one, in a section of Alabama where such work should be needed. I chose, as my field of labor, Snow Hill, the place from which I had gone to enter school at Tuskegee.

The school is now known as the Snow Hill Normal and Industrial Institute, and is located in the very center of the "Black Belt" of the State of Alabama. This is a much-used term; it is not applicable, however, to every Southern State, neither does it apply to every county in any one State. It is only to certain counties in certain States to which it may properly be applied. Wilcox and the seven adjoining counties constitute one of these sections in Alabama. The latest cen-

UPLIFTING THE SUBMERGED

sus shows that these eight counties have a colored population of 201,539, and a white population of 69,915.

Alabama has sixty-seven counties, with a total colored population of 827,307. Thus it will be seen that one-eighth of the counties contain one-fourth of the entire colored population. Because the colored people outnumber the white people in such great proportion, this is called the "Black Belt" of the State. These counties lie in the valley of the Alabama River, and constitute the most fertile section of the State.

During the early settlement of the State, white men coming into these fertile counties not only would settle as much land as a family of four or five in number could cultivate, but as much as they were able to buy Negroes to cultivate. Quite a few families with only five or six in number would have land enough to work from 100 to 1,000 Negroes. One can see from this how a few white families would, as they often did, own a whole county. Now the Negro is not migratory in his nature; having been brought to these counties during slavery, he has remained here in freedom. He is not, therefore, primarily responsible for his being here in such great numbers. These white families settled in little villages seven or eight miles apart. The distances between were made up of their plantations, on which were thousands of slaves. Only a few Negroes were employed as domestics in comparison with the great numbers who worked on plantations. It was only these few who, in learning to serve the white man, properly got a glimpse of real home life. The masses had absolutely no idea of such a life; nothing was done that would lead them to secure any such knowledge.

Since their emancipation the masses of these people have had neither competent preachers nor teachers; consequently most of them have remained hopelessly ignorant even until this day. One hearing the great condemnation heaped upon the Negro in these sections for his failure to measure up to the standards of true citizenship and to proper standards of life would get the idea that the proud Anglo-Saxon has spent a great deal of time in trying to teach him the fundamental principles that underlie life; but this is not the case. There are exceptions to all rules, however, and here and there one may find noble and patriotic white men laboring for the uplift of fallen humanity without regard to race, color, or previous condition.

UPLIFTING THE SUBMERGED

During the summer of 1893, after returning from Tuskegee, being anxious to learn more of the real condition of our people in the "Black Belt," I visited most of the places in Wilcox County and a few places in the counties of Monroe, Butler, Dallas, and Lowndes, making the entire journey on foot.

It was a bright and beautiful morning in June when I started from my home, a log cabin. More than two hundred Negroes were in the near-by fields plowing corn, hoeing cotton, and singing those beautiful songs often referred to as plantation melodies. Notably, I am Going to Roll in my Jesus' Arms; O Freedom! Before I'd be a Slave I'd be Carried to My Grave, etc., may be mentioned. With the beautiful fields of corn and cotton outstretched before me, and the shimmering brook like a silver thread twining its way through the golden meadows, and then through verdant fields, giving water to thousands of creatures as it passed, I felt that the earth was truly clothed in His beauty and the fulness of His glory.

But I had scarcely gone beyond the limits of the field when I came to a thick undergrowth of pines. Here we saw old pieces of timber and two posts.

TUSKEGEE AND ITS PEOPLE

"This marks the old cotton-gin house," said Uncle Jim, my companion, and then his countenance grew sad; after a sigh he said: "I have seen many a Negro whipped within an inch of his life at these posts. I have seen them whipped so badly that they had to be carried away in wagons. Many never did recover."

From this our road led first up-hill, then down, and finally through a stretch of woods until we reached Carlowville. This was once the most aristocratic village of the southern part of Dallas County. Perhaps no one who owned less than a hundred slaves was able to secure a home within its borders. Here still are to be seen the stately mansions of the Lydes, the Lees, the Wrumphs, the Bibbses, the Youngbloods, and the Reynoldses. Many of these mansions have been partly rebuilt and remodeled to conform to modern styles of architecture, while others have been deserted and are now fast decaying. Usually these mansions are occupied by others than the original families. The original families have sold out or have died out.

In Carlowville stands the largest white church in Dallas or Wilcox Counties. It has a seating capacity of 1,000, excluding the balcony, which, during slavery, was used exclusively for the Negroes of the families attending.

Our stay in Carlowville was necessarily short, as the evening sun was low and the nearest place for lodging was two miles ahead. Before reaching this place we came to a large one-room log cabin, 30 feet by 36 feet, on the road-side, with a double door and three holes for windows cut in the sides. There was no chimney nor anything to show that the room could be heated in cold weather. This was the Hope-well Baptist Church. Here 500 members congregated one Sunday in each month and spent the entire day in eating, shouting, and "praising God for His goodness toward the children of men." Here also the three months' school was taught during the winter. A few hundred yards beyond this church brought us to the home of a Deacon Jones.

He was living in the house occupied by the overseer of the plantation during slavery. It was customary for Deacon Jones to care for strangers who chanced to come into the community, especially for the preachers and teachers. So here we found rest.

His family consisted of himself, his wife, and six children—two boys and four girls. Mrs. Jones was noted for her ability to prepare food well, and in a short while invited us to a delicious supper of fried chicken, fried ham, some very fine homemade sugar-cane sirup, and an abundance of milk and butter. At supper Deacon Jones told of the many preachers he had entertained and their fondness for chicken.

After supper I spent some time in trying to find out the real condition of the people in this section. Mr. Jones told me how, for ten years, he had been trying to buy some land, and had been kept from it more than once, but that he was still hopeful of getting the right deeds for the land for which he had paid. He also told of many families who had recently moved into this community. These newcomers had made a good start for the year and had promising crops, but they were compelled to mortgage their growing crops in order to get " advances " for the year.

When asked of the schools, he said that there were more than five hundred children of school age in his township, but not more than two hundred of these had attended school the previous winter, and most of these for a period not longer than six weeks. He also said that the people were very indifferent as to the necessity of schoolhouses and churches.

UPLIFTING THE SUBMERGED

Quite a few who cleared a little money the previous year had spent it all in buying whisky, in gambling, in buying cheap jewelry, and for other useless articles. After spending two hours in such talk I retired for the evening. Thus ended the first day of my search for first-hand information.

We had a fine night's rest. Mr. Jones was up at early dawn to feed his horses and cattle, and before the sun was up he was out on his farm. Mrs. Jones and one of the daughters were left to prepare breakfast, and soon they, too, were ready to join the others on the farm. We took advantage of this early rising and were soon off on our journey.

Instead of going farther northward, we turned our course westward for the town of Tilden, which is only eight miles west of Snow Hill. The road from Carlowville to Tilden is somewhat hilly, but a very pleasant one, and for miles the large oak-trees formed an almost perfect arch.

On reaching Tilden we learned that there would be a union meeting of two of the churches that night. I decided that this would give me an opportunity to study the religious life of these people for myself. The members of churches No. 1 and No. 2 assembled at their respective places at eight o'clock. The members of church No. 2 had a short praise-service, and formed a line of procession to march to church No. 1. All the women of the congregation had their heads bound in pieces of white cloth, and they sang their peculiar songs as they marched. When the members of church No. 2 were within a few hundred yards of church No. 1, the singing then alternated, and finally, when the members of church No. 2 came to church No. 1, they marched around this church three times before entering it. After entering, six sermons were preached to the two congregations by six different ministers, and at least three of these could not read a word in the Bible. Each minister occupied at least one hour. Their texts were as often taken from Webster's blue-back speller as from the Bible, and sometimes this would be held upside down. It was about two o'clock in the morning when the services were concluded.

Here, again, we found no schoolhouses, and the three months' school had been taught in one of the little churches.

The next day we started for Camden, a distance of sixteen miles. This section between Tilden and Camden is perhaps the most fertile section of land in the State of Alabama. Taking a

UPLIFTING THE SUBMERGED

southwest course from Tilden, I crossed into Wilcox County again, where I saw acres of corn and miles of cotton, all being cultivated by Negroes.

The evening was far advanced when we reached Camden, but having been there before, we had no difficulty in securing lodging. Camden is the seat of Wilcox County, and has a population of about three thousand inhabitants.

The most costly buildings of the town were the court-house and jail, and these occupied the most conspicuous places.

Here great crowds of Negroes would gather on Saturdays to spend their earnings of the week for a fine breakfast or dinner on the following Sunday, or for useless trivialities.

On Saturday evenings, on the roads leading to and from Camden, as from other towns, could be seen groups of Negroes gambling here and there, and buying and selling whisky. As the county had voted against licensing whisky-selling, this was a violation of the law, and often the commission merchant, a Negro, was imprisoned for the offense, while those who supplied him went free.

In Camden I found one Negro schoolhouse; this was a box-like cottage, 20 by 16 feet, and was supposed to seat more than one hundred students.

TUSKEGEE AND ITS PEOPLE

This school, like those taught in the churches, was open only three months in the year.

After a two days' stay in Camden I next visited Miller's Ferry; this is on the Alabama River, twelve miles west of Camden. The road from Camden is one of the best roads in the State, and for miles and miles one could see nothing but cotton and corn.

At Miller's Ferry a Negro schoolhouse of ample proportions had been built on Judge Henderson's plantation. Here the school ran seven months in the year, and the colored people in the community were prosperous and showed a remarkable degree of intelligence. Their church was equally as attractive as their schoolhouse.

Judge Henderson was for twelve years Probate Judge of Wilcox County. He proved to be one of the best judges this county has ever had, and even unto this day he is admired by all, both white and black, rich and poor, for his honesty, integrity, and high sense of justice. From Judge Henderson's place we traveled southward to Rockwest, a distance of more than fifteen miles. During this journey hundreds of Negroes were seen at work in the corn- and cotton-fields. These people were almost wholly ignorant, as they had neither

UPLIFTING THE SUBMERGED

schools nor teachers, and their ministers were almost wholly illiterate.

At Rock-west I found a very intelligent colored man who had attended school at Selma, Ala., for a few years. He owned his home and ran a small grocery. He told of the hardships with which he had to contend in building up his business, and of the almost hopeless condition of the Negroes about there. He said that they usually made money each year, but that they did not know how to keep it. The merchants would induce them to buy buggies, machines, clocks, etc., but would never encourage them to buy homes. We were very much pleased with the reception which Mr. Darrington gave us, and felt very much like putting into practise our State motto, "Here We Rest," at his home, but our objective point for the day was Fatama, sixteen miles away.

On our journey that afternoon we saw hundreds of Negro one-room log cabins. Some of these were located in the dense swamps and some on the hills, while others were miles away from the public road. Most of these people had never seen a locomotive. We reached Fatama about seven o'clock that night, and here for the first time we were compelled to divide our crowd in order to get a night's lodging. Each of us had to spend the night in a one-room cabin. It was my privilege to spend the night with Uncle Jake, a jovial old man, a local celebrity. After telling him of our weary journey, he immediately made preparation for me to retire. This was done by cutting off my bed from the remainder of the cabin by hanging up a sheet on a screen. While somewhat inconvenient, my rest that night was pleasant, and the next morning found me very much refreshed and ready for another day's journey. Our company assembled at Uncle Jake's for breakfast, after which we started for Pineapple.

We found the condition of the Negroes between Fatama and Pineapple much the same as that of those we had seen the previous day. No schoolhouse was to be seen, but occasionally we would see a church at the cross-roads. We reached Pineapple late in the afternoon.

From Pineapple we went to Greenville, and from Greenville to Fort Deposit, and from Fort Deposit we returned to Snow Hill, after having traveled a distance of 157 miles and visiting four counties.

In three of these counties there is a colored population of 42,810 between the ages of five and

UPLIFTING THE SUBMERGED

twenty years, and a white population of 7,608 of the same ages. In fact, the Negro school population of Wilcox and the seven adjoining counties is as follows: Wilcox, 11,623; Dallas, 18,292; Lowndes, 13,044; Monroe, 5,615; Butler, 5,924; Marengo, 12,362; Clark, 6,898; Perry, 10,723; making a total of 85,499. Speaking of public schools in the sense that educators use the term, the colored people in this section have none. Of course, there are so-called public schools here and there, running from three to five months in the year and paying the teachers from $7.50 to $18 per month; but the teachers are incompetent, and the schools are usually in the hands of those not too much interested in the cause of education. Many of these trustees do not visit the schools once in ten years, and they know absolutely nothing of the methods of discipline even used by the teachers.

Our trip through this section revealed the following facts: (1) That while many opportunities were denied our people, they abused many privileges; (2) that there was a colored population, in this section visited, of more than 200,000, and a school population of 85,499; (3) that the people were ignorant and superstitious; (4) that the teachers and preachers for the most part were of the same condition; (5) that there were no public or private libraries and reading-rooms to which they had access; (6) that, strictly speaking, there were no public schools and only one private one. Now what can be expected of any people in such a condition? Can the blind lead the blind? They could not in the days of old, and it is not likely that they can now.

After this trip through the "Black Belt" I was more convinced than ever before of the great need of an industrial school in the very midst of these people; a school that would correct the erroneous ideas the people held of education; a school that would put most stress upon the things which the people were most likely to have to do with through life; a school that would endeavor to make education practical rather than theoretical; a school that would train men and women to be good workers, good leaders, good husbands, good wives, and finally train them to be fit citizens of the State, and proper subjects for the kingdom of God.

With this idea the Snow Hill Normal and Industrial Institute was started ten years ago in an old, dilapidated, one-room log cabin with one teacher, three students, and no State appropriation, and without any church or society responsible

UPLIFTING THE SUBMERGED

for one dollar of its expenses. Aside from this unfortunate state of affairs, the condition of the people was most miserable. This was due partly to poor crops and partly to bad management on their part.

In many instances the tenants were not only unable to pay their debts, but were also unable to pay their rents. In a few cases the landlords had to provide, at their own expense, provisions for their tenants. This was simply another way of establishing soup-houses on the plantations. The idea of buying land was foreign to all of them, and there were not more than twenty acres of land owned by the colored people in this whole neighborhood. The churches and schools were practically closed, while crime and immorality were rampant. The carrying of men and women to the chain-gang was a frequent occurrence. Aside from all this, these people believed that the end of education was to free their children from manual labor rather than prepare them for more and better work. They were very much opposed to industrial education. When the school was started, many of the parents came to the school and forbade our " working " their children, stating as their objection that their children had been working all their lives, and they did not mean to send them to school to learn to work. Not only did they forbid our having their children work, but many took their children out of school rather than have them do so. A good deal of this opposition was kept up by illiterate preachers and incompetent teachers, here and there, who had not had any particular training for their profession. In fact, ninety-eight per cent of them had attended no school. We continued, however, to keep the " industrial plank " in our platform, and year after year some additional industry was added until we now have thirteen industries in constant operation. Agriculture is the foremost and basic industry of the institution. We do this because we are in a farming section and ninety-five per cent of the people in this section depend upon some form of agriculture for a livelihood. How changed are the conditions now as regards our work! From the little one-room log cabin, the school has grown so that it now owns 100 acres of land, 14 buildings, counting large and small, with property valued at $37,000. From three students, it has grown so that we now have a school with more than four hundred students annually in attendance, representing more than a dozen Alabama counties and seven States. It has

UPLIFTING THE SUBMERGED

also grown from one to twenty teachers and officers. Including the class that graduated last term, thirty-seven have finished the course. All are living but one. No charge of criminal wrong-doing has been brought against even one of them. One of the young women is married to the head teacher, another to the superintendent of industries, and seven other graduates are employed in responsible positions by the school. One of these has taken a special course at Harvard University, three have taken additional courses at Tuskegee, one is in charge of the woman's department of a large school in Mississippi, two have founded schools of their own, one at Tilden, Ala., the other at Greensboro, Ala. All have remained in the country among the masses whom they are helping to uplift, and most of them in Wilcox County, the county in which the school is located. Of the thirty-seven graduates, twenty-seven own their own homes. Aside from the graduates, about five hundred others have been under the influence of the school for a longer or shorter period; many of these are making exceptionally good records.

The growth on the part of the people has kept corresponding pace with the growth of the institution. The farmers, who ten years ago depended wholly on the landlords for food supplies, have grown to be independent, raising most of their own supplies. They are rapidly passing from the renters' class to the owners' class; they are possessing themselves of the soil. This may be seen from the fact that ten years ago they owned in this county but twenty acres of land; to-day they own 4,000 acres of land. Many of the most prosperous farmers have opened bank-accounts. The people no longer oppose industrial education; they now refuse to send their children to any school where they can not secure some industrial education.

For our part we find it wholly impossible to accommodate all who come to us from time to time to take the trades' instruction. The churches hereabout have been revived, new and better schoolhouses have been built, and the county school terms extended in many cases from two and three to five and six months; competent teachers and preachers, both intellectually and morally, have been employed. Crime and immorality are being uprooted, and virtue and civic righteousness are being planted in their stead. The commercial and economic conditions have improved in every way, and there was never a more cordial relation existing be-

UPLIFTING THE SUBMERGED

tween the races in this section than now. With these things true, the one-room log cabin can not survive, and is rapidly giving way to houses having three, four, and, in some places, six and seven rooms.

After having been here at Snow Hill for a few years, we felt that while we were helping the children in the class-room, something should be done to help the parents; so we organized what we call the Snow Hill Negro Conference, on January 13, 1897. This conference is modeled after the famous Tuskegee Negro Conferences, and meets once a year. At this conference the farmers from this and the adjoining counties come together. There were 500 at our last conference. The school is almost wholly given up to farmers on Conference day. Here we listen to educational, religious, moral, and financial reports from many sections. Those who have succeeded, tell the others how they have done so, and those who have not succeeded tell how they are trying to succeed. From these annual meetings the farmers get new ideas, new information, and take fresh courage; they return to their farms more determined to succeed than ever before. When we commenced these meetings the reports were discouraging, and from many sections the condition of the race thereabout seemed hopeless. Many said that in the same section they could not buy land at any price. There were only twenty acres of land reported at the first conference. At the last one, reports showed that the people had purchased more than four thousand acres since the beginning of these conferences seven years ago. At our first meeting the reports showed that the one-room log-cabin home was the rule; at our last meeting it had become the exception. These conferences have tried all along to induce the people to raise more of their own food-supplies. We also waged a ceaseless war upon the one-room log-cabin home, which has resulted in almost annihilating them. This war shall never cease until there is not a one-room log cabin left in all this section. The one-room log cabin is a pestilent menace to decent living.

Following the farmers' conference, we have the workers' conference during vacation. This conference is chiefly composed of teachers and preachers, and represents an idea got from Tuskegee. In this conference we get a clear idea of what the teachers and preachers are doing, the methods they are pursuing, and the results being achieved. The teachers are encouraged to make

UPLIFTING THE SUBMERGED

education less theoretical and more practical; the preachers are urged to preach to our people less of the dying religion and more of the living religion. While they are encouraged to build better schoolhouses and churches, they are also reminded of the fact that these are not the ends, but only the means to an end; that they are only of value in proportion as they can be used to build up a hopeful and noble life in the communities where they are located. However much the material side may be held up to them, they are told that in the last analysis the spiritual is always the end. The reports at our last Workers' Conference were most encouraging. Wherever the intelligent teacher and preacher have gone, the condition of the people has been improved. To my mind this demonstrates most clearly that the great need of our people is intelligent leaders, and it is this that we ask for; it is this for which Snow Hill is striving. While much good is being accomplished through the Workers' Conference, the "Black Belt Improvement Society," which I have organized, deals more directly with the people in our immediate neighborhood. The aim of this society is clearly set forth in its constitution, a part of which is as follows:

TUSKEGEE AND ITS PEOPLE

1. This society shall be known as the Black Belt Improvement Society. Its object shall be the general uplift of the people of the Black Belt of Alabama; to make them better morally, mentally, spiritually, and financially.

2. It shall be the object of the Black Belt Improvement Society to, as far as possible, eliminate the credit system from our social fabric; to stimulate in all members the desire to raise, as far as possible, all their food supplies at home, and pay cash for whatever may be purchased at the stores.

3. To bring about a system of cooperation in the purchase of what supplies can not be raised at home wherever it can be done to advantage.

4. To discuss topics of interest to the communities in which the various societies may be organized, and topics relating to the general welfare of the race, and especially to farmers.

5. To teach the people to practise the strictest economy, and especially to obtain and diffuse such information among farmers as shall lead to the improvement and diversification of crops, in order to create in farmers a desire for homes and better home conditions, and to stimulate a love for labor in both old and young. Each local organization may offer small prizes for the cleanest and best-kept house, the best pea-patch, and the best ear of corn, etc.

6. To aid each other in sickness and in death;

UPLIFTING THE SUBMERGED

for this purpose a fee of ten cents will be collected from each member every month and held sacred, to be used for no other purpose whatever.

7. It shall be one of the great objects of this society to stimulate its members to acquire homes, and urge those who already possess homes to improve and beautify them.

8. To urge our members to purchase only the things that are absolutely necessary.

9. To exert our every effort to obliterate those evils which tend to destroy our character and our homes, such as intemperance, gambling, and social impurity.

10. To refrain from spending money and time foolishly or in unprofitable ways; to take an interest in the care of our highways, in the paying of our taxes, and the education of our children; to plant shade trees, repair our yard fences, and in general, as far as possible, bring our home life up to the highest standards of civilization.

This society has several standing committees, as follows: on government, on education, on business, on housekeeping, on labor, and on farming. The chairman of these respective committees holds monthly meetings in the various communities, at which time various topics pertaining to the welfare and uplift of the people are discussed. As a result of these meetings the people return to their homes with new inspiration. These meetings are doing good in the communities where they are being held, and our sincere hope is that such meetings may be extended. The ills that most retard the Negroes of the rural South are sought to be reached by the school and by the several organizations which have been organized by it. These articles of the simple constitution go to the very bottom of the conditions.

If one would again take the trip which I made in the summer of 1893, he would find that two-thirds of the land lying between Snow Hill and Carlowville, a distance of seven miles, is now owned and controlled entirely by Negroes. In Carlowville, instead of the old one-room-cabin church, there is a beautiful church with glass windows. An acre of land has been bought, and a neat and comfortable schoolhouse with glass windows has been erected, and a graduate of my school is the teacher. Many families in that section are now owning homes. A great revolution is also taking place in Tilden. John Thomas, one of our graduates, Class of '01, has gone into this place, induced the people to buy thirty acres of land, on which they have erected a splendid building having two rooms, and

UPLIFTING THE SUBMERGED

the school is being conducted seven months in the year. Many farmers in this section are now owning homes, some of them owning as much as 400 acres of land. This improvement is steadily going on in all sections where the influence of our school has reached.

Thus it will be seen that the work in the classroom is only a small part of what we are trying to do for the uplift of the Negro people in the Black Belt.

In order that this good work may be pushed more rapidly, it is necessary that we give some time to this particular movement. This can only be done by our having here a strong and healthy institution with an endowment sufficiently large to relieve us of our great financial burden. An adequate endowment would meet this need. While we are anxious to raise an endowment fund, our burden could be partially relieved by the school securing possession of a large plantation in the neighborhood which is now, and has been for three years, offered to us. This plantation contains between three thousand and four thousand acres of land, and can be bought for $30,000, and would afford us unbounded opportunity for the extension of the agricultural features of our work, which would enable us to raise more, if not all, of our food supplies.

I have tried as simply as possible in this article to state the real condition of the people in the Black Belt section of this State, and to tell how we are trying to cope with these conditions. Our constant feeling is that there is so much to be done, and that so little has been accomplished.

In closing: The inspiration derived at Tuskegee; the instruction given in shop, and field, and class-room; the guiding hand of its illustrious Principal—all of these have had their impress upon me and have urged me to dedicate myself unreservedly to these people, among whom I was reared, among whom I shall continue to labor, among whom I shall at the last be buried.

XI

A DAIRYMAN'S STORY

By Lewis A. Smith

In any attempt to write a story of my life and work, the " work " feature must predominate.

I was born March 27, 1877, at Louisville, Ky. My father and mother were slaves of old Georgia stock. My father, after freedom, was for a time permitted to attend Howard University, Washington, D. C. He was a candy-maker. My mother attended Atlanta University.

In 1878 my parents left Atlanta, where my two brothers were born, and located in Louisville. Leaving Louisville in 1881, the family moved to Chicago, Ill., where I lived until I entered Tuskegee Institute, of which my mother and I had heard much.

After reaching Chicago, my parents established a confectionery store. My earlier days were mostly spent behind the counter in the store, not as a clerk helping to earn profits, but in an endeavor to make profits disappear. I was much in love with the nice things we had for sale.

An unfortunate family "incident" in 1882 resulted in placing my two brothers and me in the custody of my mother. Our childhood pleasures were marred by this affair. Although I was too young to fully understand the situation, I realized that I lacked the pleasures that other children had; I realized the absence of that paternal care and affection that other children enjoyed— the home was not complete. I can not recall my childhood with any special pleasure.

I entered the public schools of Chicago when I was seven years of age. I made a very good record in my studies, attested by the fact that I made two grades the first year, and one grade with excellent marks each succeeding year thereafter. My deportment was not exemplary. I can remember occasions when I was severely reprimanded for being absent from school without an excuse, having gone fishing, or bathing in Lake Michigan, or skating in the parks in winter.

That was before the compulsory school law went into effect, or at least before it affected me. I was not, however, a bad boy. I was neither rough nor tough; I had no bad habits other than

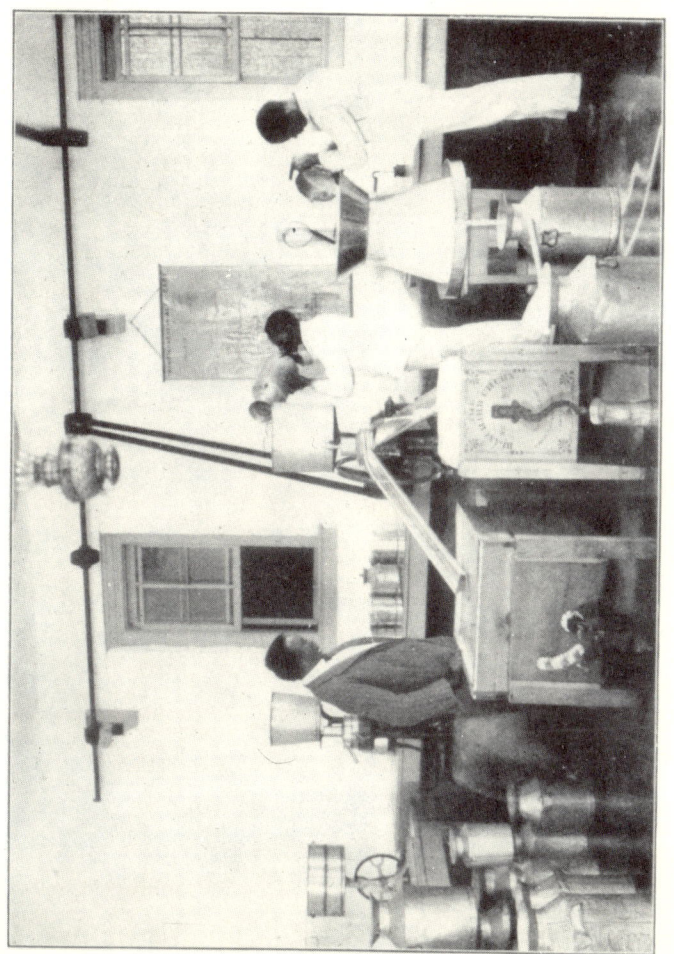

IN THE DAIRY.
Students using separators.

A DAIRYMAN'S STORY

smoking corn-silk cigarettes, and I soon stopped that as the novelty of the thing wore off. My young mind and body required recreation. Unlike the children of the South, who had three months of school and nine months of play or work in the fields, I had nine months of school and three months of play. I thought the ratio was in the wrong proportion. But as I grew older I became more settled and more interested in my studies.

Although during the greater portion of my school life in Chicago I was the sole Negro pupil in my classes, yet I do not remember a single occasion when prejudice was leveled at me by teacher or schoolmate.

Early, after throwing off my wildness, I realized the need and the advantage of possessing an education, and, having such excellent facilities at hand, determined to become educated, and diligently pursued that object. Just as I was about to enter the eighth grade, however, I had to give up going to school, and go to work.

I secured employment with a wood-engraving firm as general office- and errand-boy. My wages were $2.50 a week. About fifty cents of this sum I spent each week for car-fare and incidentals. As I lived three miles from my work it would have been necessary for me to spend my whole allowance for car-fare had I not stolen rides on railroad trains. I often wonder now how I could have jumped on and off swift-moving trains, day after day, without receiving some serious injury. Surely Providence must have protected me in my endeavor to save my scanty earnings. My clothing did not cost much, as I was the "happy" recipient of the cast-off clothes of the older members of the family.

My work was agreeable and my employer was generously sympathetic. Realizing that wood-engraving and illustrating would offer remunerative employment, I sought to learn the trade, but was told that I would have to serve an apprenticeship of six months without pay; that precluded all hope of learning that trade.

Manhood approached before I was prepared to do anything. I did not earn much in my youth, and could not expect to earn much in manhood without preparation. I then resolved to enter school again, but the expense of a thorough course was an apparently insurmountable obstacle. I had been unable to save much from my meager allowance. I had heard of the Tuskegee Institute and of the opportunities there offered to poor young men and women. I decided to enter that school.

A DAIRYMAN'S STORY

A friend helped me to purchase an excursion ticket to Atlanta, Ga., where was being held the Cotton-States and International Exposition. I left Chicago in November, and after two days spent in Atlanta with relatives and in seeing the sights, I exchanged my return coupon for a ticket to Tuskegee.

I arrived at Chehaw, the station where passengers transfer for Tuskegee, and taking passage in a wagonette, a crude substitute for our modern means of interurban transit—the little train was not running on that day—we drove through a picturesque country abounding in woods, vales, and cultivated fields, occasionally coming across landmarks of antebellum days. Here one was really in communion with Nature, so different it was from the massive specimens of architecture, the clatter of horses on the cobblestone pavement, the rattle of elevated trains, and the activity of commercial life of the Western metropolis from which I had come. As we reached high elevations glimpses of the institution came into view.

Tuskegee was a surprise to me; it surpassed my fondest hope. The majestic buildings, the monuments to the fidelity and building skill of past classes, the well-designed landscape architecture, made me feel that I had at last found the place where I could be prepared for real life. I received a cordial welcome from the teachers; also from the students, especially from those connected with the religious and literary organizations, of which there are quite a number.

When asked the industry I wished to learn, I chose that of agriculture. Like hundreds of boys confined to city environment, I had a craving for Nature, a fondness for live stock, and for all that I should come in contact with while taking that course. I worked during the daytime the first year and attended school at night, thereby acquiring experience and accumulating a credit to apply to my board when I should enter the day-school. Soon after entering the agricultural department I had made such progress that I was placed in charge of the hotbeds and grew vegetables all winter. It was a marvelous accomplishment with me, for I could not have grown them even in the summer before I entered that department. The care of the various seeds used on the farm was also in my charge.

This privilege afforded me opportunities for seed-testing and for observing plant development; it was all very instructive. While attending the aca-

A DAIRYMAN'S STORY

demic classes at night, the daytime was devoted entirely to study in the various divisions of the agricultural department.

At the expiration of my first year as a night-school student, I entered day-school, devoting about equal time to academic and agricultural classes, and a small portion of the time to the study of music, being a member of the Institute brass band, and in my last year a member of the orchestra.

During my second summer's vacation I went into the southern part of Montgomery County, Ala., in search of a school to teach. There was no schoolhouse, no school fund, nor any appropriation available except for a three months' term during the winter. After further canvass I was permitted to open a school in the little church at Strata, Ala. The large attendance of pupils and their eagerness to learn won my sympathy and I would gladly have planted a sprig of Tuskegee there had I not had strong inclinations for a commercial life. I conducted a class in agriculture for the benefit of the farmers. I believe it was helpful to them. My spare time was spent in going through the country noting the waste of the land and the lack of enterprise among the owners and tenants, due in large measure, I am sure, to the mortgage system and the deep ignorance of the people. Most of the evenings I spent listening to the terrible stories of slavery days from the lips of those who had passed through them.

In the midst of this service I received a telegram announcing the death of my mother. I was too far from home to return in time to see the last of her, even if I had had the means to do so. I was in grief; I had sustained a great loss; she was my all, my mother.

I returned to Tuskegee and graduated with the Class of '98.

I am grateful to Tuskegee Institute, to the genius of Mr. Washington, for the opportunities I had to acquire an education; to the members of the Faculty for their assistance, and to my father, who gave me much of material aid and encouragement.

After graduating, I spent two months at special work in the school dairy; then, with the assistance of my father, I secured a position with the Forest City Creamery Company of Rockford, Ill. Entering this company's employ about the 15th of August, 1898, I have been employed ever since at the same place.

The Forest City Creamery is one of the largest

A DAIRYMAN'S STORY

butter-making concerns in the United States, averaging twenty thousand pounds of butter per day. We make two grades of butter, known as process, or renovated, and creamery butter. There are employed at this plant about seventy-five persons.

My work consists in what is known to the trade as "starter-making" and preparing the flavor for the butter. The work is bacteriological, propagating a species of bacteria which produces the pleasant aroma and flavor of good butter. It requires not only an understanding of bacteriology, but skilled workmanship and earnest attention to details. The secret processes of this company are known to a close group only, of which I am one. My work here has been entirely successful and satisfactory to my employers, if I may judge from a highly complimentary interview with one of the officers of the company regarding my work, published in one of the leading daily newspapers of Rockford, and the fact that I am now receiving double my initial wages.

I have a record not surpassed by any other employee of this company. Between June 24, 1901, following a wedding-trip to Tuskegee, and August 15, 1904, when we visited the St. Louis Exposition, I have worked each day at the Creamery, including Sundays and holidays, my work requiring that I do so. These 1,155 consecutive days of labor were made possible by a total abstinence from all intoxicating liquors and tobacco. My success here can be credited to the efficient training I received at Tuskegee.

"It is not well for man to live alone." Following this injunction I have taken unto myself a helpmeet, who is all that the word implies, loving, economical, and well trained in domestic arts. Shortly after our marriage we began paying for a home of eleven rooms located in a good residence portion of the city. The lower part of the house, containing six rooms, we occupy, and have comfortably furnished; the up-stairs portion, containing five rooms, we rent to a family of white people; the rent we receive equals the interest on the investment.

We have one child, a little girl two years old, who furnishes sunshine to an already happy home.

Our house is surrounded by a lawn with shade- and fruit-trees, and many flower-beds. The back yard contains a garden with berry plants, a well-built and well-arranged poultry-house, a yard containing a flock of pure-bred fowls, the nucleus of a future enterprise, and a barn with a good

A DAIRYMAN'S STORY

horse, a buggy, etc., for our pleasure and convenience.

My ambition when leaving school was first to endeavor to become independent financially, so that I might enjoy my old age; then, if it were possible, to gain that independence early in life by economy, by earning for myself what I earn for my employer; to try to make it possible for the Negro farmer to sell his produce to the Negro gin, the Negro cotton-mill, or creamery, as the case might be; my idea being, by this community of interest, to help the Negro people about me to help themselves and their fellows. I believe, in the words of the motto of the Class of '98—my class—that " we rise upon the structure we ourselves have builded." I have tried to live with this thought ever before me.

XII

THE STORY OF A WHEELWRIGHT

By Edward Lomax

I was born in the small town of Demopolis, in the western part of the State of Alabama, January 17, 1877. My uncle was a wheelwright, and I, at an early age, was led to desire to become an artisan such as my uncle was. I interceded with him and became the " handy boy " around the shop in which he worked, and picked up much useful information; but there was nothing progressive or directly helpful in the work I was permitted to do. I also did some little work in blacksmithing while in the shop.

What to me was a fortunate circumstance was the meeting with a chance acquaintance who was returning from Tuskegee Institute for his vacation. This young man told me most glowing stories of the Tuskegee Institute. He was so enthusiastic that he imparted much of his enthusiasm to me. He himself was taking instruction in the wheelwrighting division, and could give at firsthand the information I most desired. The whole

THE STORY OF A WHEELWRIGHT

Tuskegee plan was outlined to me: how I could learn my trade, and at the same time get book instruction; how I could earn by labor enough to carry me through school while securing to myself the advantages mentioned. I had had to learn by seeing others do, and it was now pointed out to me how I could "learn by doing," and that was the thing I wanted. I had been used to being kept from the use of tools and everything that would really help me to learn wheelwrighting; the only chances I ever had being to "knock about" the shop, occasionally having some worthless job, with cast-off tools to work with, entrusted to me.

The upshot of it was that I decided to go to Tuskegee, and carefully saved as much of my wages of $2.50 per week as I possibly could, so as to purchase clothing, books, and those incidentals insisted upon by the school that each student must have. I wrote to the school, and received a letter from Principal Washington admitting me should I find myself able to meet the requirements stated as follows:

No person will be admitted to the school as a student who can not pass the examination for the C Preparatory class. To enter this class one must be able to read, write, and understand addition, subtraction, multiplication, and division.

Applicants for admission must be of good moral character and must bring at least two letters of recommendation as to their moral character from reliable persons of their communities.

The Day-School.—The Day-School is intended for those who are able to pay all or the greater part of their expenses in cash. Students attending the Day-School are required to work one day in each week and every other Saturday.

They must also be fourteen years of age, of good physique, and able to pass the examination for the C Preparatory class, as stated above.

The Night-School.—The requirements for entering the Night-School are the same as for entering the Day-School, with the additional requisites: Applicants must be fully sixteen years of age instead of fourteen, and physically able to perform an adult's labor. Cripples are under no circumstances admitted to this department.

The Night-School is designed for young men and women who earnestly desire to educate themselves, but who are too poor to pay even the small charge made in the Day-School. Students will not be admitted to the Night-School who are known to be able to enter the Day-School; and when a student has fraudulently gained admission, upon discovery of the deception, must either enter the Day-School or leave the institution.

Trades are assigned as nearly as possible in accordance with the students' desires. In assign-

THE STORY OF A WHEELWRIGHT

ing young men and women to a trade, their mental ability and intelligence to grasp it, and physical ability to perform the duties required, are all carefully considered. At the beginning of the school year it often happens that certain of the industries are quickly filled; and when this happens, applicants for this particular industry are assigned to some other division until a vacancy occurs.

The school authorities also sent me a card notifying me as to the school's requirements in the way of discipline. These seemed to me to be rather overexacting, but I resolved to try to live up to them if I should be admitted. Among these were the following:

The rules governing the school are aimed to be those which best promote the welfare and happiness of all.

Each student is required to have a Bible.

Regular habits of rest and recreation are required.

No student is allowed to leave the grounds without permission.

Male students when permitted to leave the grounds must wear the regulation cap.

No young woman is permitted to leave the grounds of the institution unless accompanied by a teacher.

The Institute has adequate facilities for bathing, and all students are required to bathe at stated periods. Bath-houses for young men and young women, with swimming-pools and shower-bath appointments, afford every facility in this regard.

The use of intoxicating drinks and the use of tobacco are strictly forbidden.

Dice-playing and card-playing are strictly prohibited.

Students are liable to be dropped for inability to master their studies, irregularity of attendance, or for failure to comply with the regulations of the school after due notice.

The demeriting system has been adopted by the school as the principal method of discipline for misconduct: $33\frac{1}{3}$ demerit marks constitute a "warning," and upon receiving three warnings a student is liable to suspension or expulsion, according as the Executive Council may determine.

All non-resident students are expected to board on the school-grounds, unless there is some good reason for a contrary arrangement.

Students are not registered for a shorter period than one month; those who leave before the end of a month are charged for a full month's board.

When students desire to leave the school they are required to have parents or guardian write directly to the Principal for permission to do so.

The Dean of the Woman's Department meets all the young women of the school each Friday

THE STORY OF A WHEELWRIGHT

afternoon, and the Commandant all of the young men every Saturday evening, at which times talks, both instructive and corrective, are given. No student is excused from these meetings except by special permission.

Students who sign a contract to work a specified time at some trade or other work must be released from their contract before application for an excuse from school will be considered. Any student leaving without a written excuse will not be allowed to return, and students under contract will not only be dismissed, but will forfeit whatever cash there may be to their credit in the school treasury. Students must settle their accounts before leaving.

Remittances in payment of bills should be made to the Principal or Treasurer (and not to the student) by post-office money-order, registered letter, or check.

Students are not allowed to retain firearms in their possession. The Commandant of Cadets will retain and give receipts for any brought.

Low or profane language will subject students to severe discipline. Students are liable to reprimand, confinement, or other punishment.

Letter-writing is subject to regulation, and all mail- and express-packages are inspected and contents noted. Students are urged to write their parents at least once a week.

Wardrobes and rooms of students are subject

to inspection and regulation by proper officers at all times, and regular and thorough inspection of same are made from time to time.

I was admitted in due course of time.

I reached Tuskegee on the 5th of September, 1896, and after purchasing books, etc., my "cash assets," $12, were about exhausted. I could not enter as a day-school student, as I did not have the money to do so. In the night-school I found a chance which I gladly embraced. As I had desired, I was assigned to the wheelwright division for two years, signing a formal contract to that effect. I spent the whole of each day in the shop, attended industrial or theory classes two afternoons in each week, besides taking mechanical drawing (as all trades students are required to do), and attended evening classes.

I applied myself as earnestly as I possibly could, and lost no time in getting right down to business. So well had I done that, that when a call reached the school during the spring of 1897 for a competent blacksmith, I was sent to do the work. I was excused from school on April 15th of that year and went to Shorter's, Ala., a settlement about eighteen miles from Tuskegee. I remained there until October.

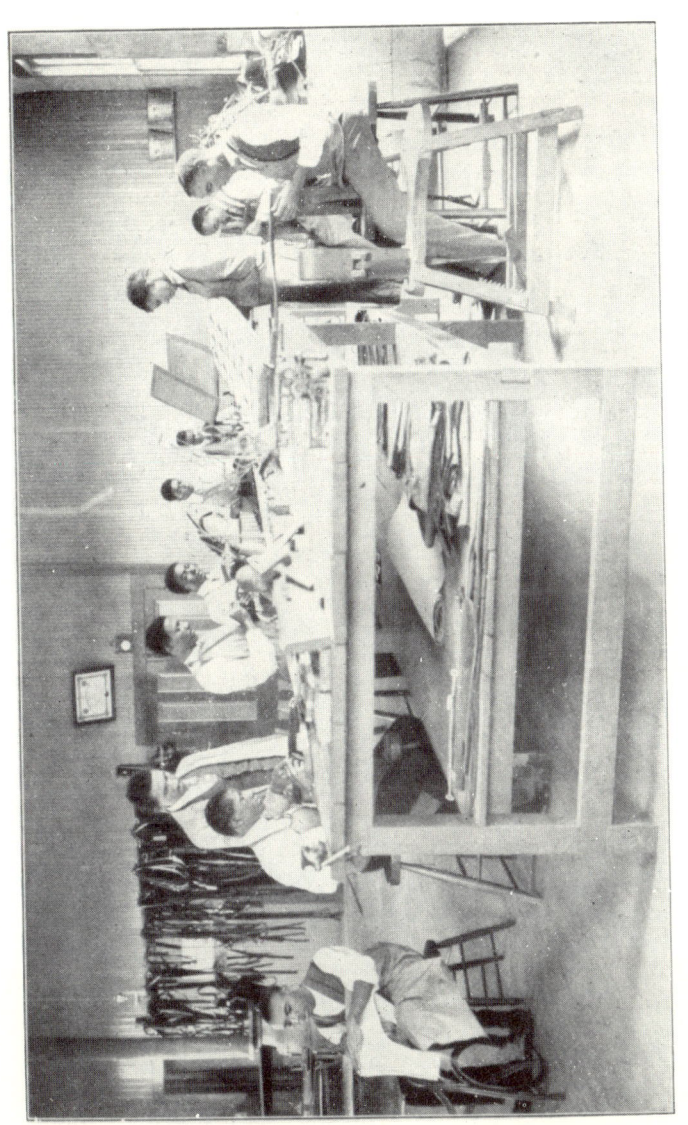

STUDENTS AT WORK IN THE HARNESS-SHOP.

THE STORY OF A WHEELWRIGHT

In a way, I regarded that period somewhat as a vacation period, as I did not lose much time from my classes. The surroundings were pleasant and profitable, and I had a chance to enter into the life of the people and help them a great deal. While there I earned enough money to send for my brother and enter him in Tuskegee, that he might have the same chance I was enjoying to get an education. I wanted my brother to enter the blacksmith-shop, as I saw visions of a blacksmithing and wheelwrighting business to be owned and conducted by Lomax Brothers some time in the future. I also provided clothing out of what I had earned for both my brother and myself.

At close of the school term in 1898 I was able to secure employment at Uniontown, Ala., with Messrs. J. L. Dykes and Company, doing a general wheelwrighting and blacksmithing business—the largest business of its kind in the town. I remained at Uniontown, working for the firm until October, when I again returned to Tuskegee. The sum per day I received was a most flattering tribute to Tuskegee's ability to take a stiff country lad like myself, and turn him, in a few months, into a workman commanding decent wages.

What this means to the masses of the students

who go to Tuskegee the general public can have no idea. It is a great thing for a boy who never earned more than the merest pittance a day to go to a school where he can secure an education by working for it, and at the same time be fitted to earn wages, as many of them do, three and even five times as high as before going there. This accounts, in a large measure I am sure, for the fact that so large a number refuse to remain and go through the full courses of academic study.

Many of them, finding themselves able in a few months to earn sums far beyond any previous hope, decide to take advantage at once of this increased earning capacity; but since the work is so well graded, no boy can get his trade without getting, at the same time, academic instruction, and instruction in those character-forming things all about the student at Tuskegee.

I began the new term with $50, which sum was to my credit in the school treasury, having been earned by my labor.

During the summer of 1899 I was again offered work at Uniontown by Messrs. J. L. Dykes and Company. I remained with them only two months, however. Afterward I worked at

THE STORY OF A WHEELWRIGHT

the McKinley Brothers' Wagon Factory at Demopolis, Ala.; as a journeyman workman at Tuskegee, in the Institute's Wheelwrighting Shop, and with the Nack Carriage Company at Mobile, Ala., the largest shop of its kind in that city and one of the largest in the whole South, a firm doing strictly high-grade work. In all of these positions I have every reason to believe that I gave full and complete satisfaction. While with the last-named company I won the personal favor and interest of the manager and continued to study. He recommended that I add to my Tuskegee training by taking the correspondence course of the Technical School for Carriage Draftsmen and Mechanics, New York. I remained with this firm until I was offered a position by Mr. R. R. Taylor, the present director of mechanical industries of the Tuskegee Institute, three years ago. I was greatly pleased and flattered when I was called to take charge of the division in which I had received my own instruction. Since being at Tuskegee I have continued to study, and am satisfied that I have well used my opportunities.

This division over which I preside is located on the first floor of the Trades Building. It is well fitted for work in general wheelwrighting and repairing.

Included in the equipment are ten woodworkers' benches 32 inches high, 42 inches wide, and 8 feet long. Each bench is divided into two parts, making it possible for two persons to work at the same bench without interference. The benches have three drawers and one closet on each side, in which tools used by the students are kept.

Each pupil is provided with the following tools: One coach-maker's vise, one 26-inch No. 6 cross-cut saw, one 12-inch back saw, one set of planes, one set of chisels, one set of auger-bits, one set of gimlet-bits, one ratchet-brace, one coach-maker's drawing-knife, one spoke-shave, one thumb-gauge, one try-square, one bevel, one hammer, and one mallet. Other tools are kept in reserve by the instructor and are used only when needed.

The division is constantly building new work, such as wagons, drays, horse- and hand-carts, wheelbarrows, buggies, and road-carts. The work of repairing vehicles and farm implements for the school, and a large amount of repairing for the locality, is done by my students. The course is as follows:

THE STORY OF A WHEELWRIGHT

The First Year.—Care of shop, names and care of tools, general measurements; elementary work with saw, plane, drawing-knife, chisel, and spoke-shave; practise in the making and application of joints, i. e., splices, mortises, tenons, and miters; kinds of wood used and how to select; practise-work on parts of wagons and bodies; Industrial Classes and Mechanical Drawing during the year.

The Second Year.—Pattern-making, working by patterns, practise-work on parts of wagons continued; making wheelbarrows and hand-carts, repairing wagons; practise in wheel-building; construction of wagons, carts, and drays; practise on parts of buggies and wagons; industrial classes and Mechanical Drawing during the year.

The Third Year.—Building wheels; general repairs on buggies and wagons continued; practise-work on parts of buggies, phaetons, farm- and business-wagons; shop economics, estimates, bills of material; industrial classes and Mechanical Drawing during the year.

The student in wheelwrighting receives instruction in wood-turning; the course is the same as that given to students in carpentry.

I was married late last summer, 1904, and am now living at Tuskegee as a member of the Faculty of the school I entered as a raw recruit.

XIII

THE STORY OF A BLACKSMITH

By Jubie B. Bragg

BOTH my mother and father were compelled to work in the field as farmers. They had four children, all now living, of whom I am the eldest. I was born in Twiggs County, Ga., February 17, 1876, but in 1881 the family moved to Macon, Ga., where they lived until 1886. The cruelest possible blow befell us when both mother and father died in April of that year, within ten days of each other.

My parents were intelligent, and though they had had no opportunities for securing an education, yet they were able to teach their children the alphabet and how to spell a few simple words. My first lessons were in Webster's blue-back speller, so when I started to school at six years of age I was not the dullest boy beginning at the same place, because of the instruction I had received. I first went to a Miss Mary Tom, who taught in St. Paul's Church in East Macon. I went there but one school session. I was next sent to a Miss Carr,

THE STORY OF A BLACKSMITH

who taught in the basement of the Presbyterian church on Washington Avenue, West Macon. To her, also, I only went one term. I was next started in Lewis' High School, now known as Ballard's Normal School, but was soon compelled to cease going there because of the death of both parents, as already mentioned, in April of that same term.

I was now but ten years of age. My aunt took charge of me and of the other children. I was immediately "hired out" to a family named Horton, for my victuals and clothing. I worked for this family about six months, all of whom were kind to me, especially Mr. Horton, Jr., who at this time had charge of an ice-house. Each day I carried his meals to him and could confidently count upon receiving from him a nickel (five cents), which was forthwith invested in candy as I returned. It was a real pleasure to meet and make myself known to Mr. Horton, Jr., the young man who had been so kind to me in Birmingham, Ala., in 1901, after my graduation from Tuskegee. He was apparently glad to see me, and especially to learn that I had been attending the Tuskegee Institute. After leaving the Horton family I went to work in a grocery store, that of a Mrs. Machold, from whom I received $4 a month for my services. I only remained with her a short while.

The work I liked best of all, however, was that with the shoe firm of Bearden and Brantley. I had my Sundays, and was off from work at six o'clock each week-day—a great change from my former employment.

When I was twelve years of age I went to visit an uncle who lived in Baldwin County, Ga. I had gone to remain two weeks; as a matter of fact I was with him three years. I worked on the farm every day while with him, and went to school about two months each year. In this short time I was only able to review the lessons I had already had. After returning to Macon, a number of young men who had been to Tuskegee persuaded me to consider going there to school. The most strenuous opposition came from my own relatives. After many conversations about the matter I had finally to go against their will. They honestly felt that such reading and writing as I could do was quite enough education for me, or for any other Negro boy.

I reached the school, after being properly admitted, on the 11th of September, 1893, and registered as a student in the night-school, as I

THE STORY OF A BLACKSMITH

had no money, and could pay in cash for no part of my expenses. I was assigned, after examination, to the A Preparatory class. I was assigned work at the barns, fed cows, milked, and rendered such other service as was required by the instructor.

Soon after reaching Tuskegee and after I had begun " working out " my expenses, I learned that the officers of the school were contemplating a new scheme whereby all of the students in the night-school would work one-half of each day, go to school one-half of each day, and pay $4 a month in cash into the school treasury. Mrs. Washington, the " guardian angel " of the student body at Tuskegee called me and several other students into conference and asked us to frankly state how the new schedule would affect us, what we thought of the plan, how much money we were able to pay, etc. Out of the whole number only four declared they were able to pay the $4 a month; the larger number, like myself, were utterly unable to pay anything in cash, being dependent absolutely upon our ability to cover our expenses by work in some of the industrial divisions. It was finally decided to forego this contemplated arrangement, and I, and the majority of others situated like myself, were made very happy. My

TUSKEGEE AND ITS PEOPLE

whole future hinged on this decision, as I should have been compelled to leave school if it had been put in operation. I remained at the school during the summer of 1894, the school very kindly arranging each summer to keep a large number of students and providing work for them. It was to me an advantage to remain. I had no money for railroad fare, and I was sure of securing a trade, wheelwrighting, at the beginning of the next term. I had desired to go into the blacksmith-shop, but it was so crowded that there was no reasonable assurance that I should be able to secure entrance thereto.

At the beginning of the fall term, 1894, I entered the wheelwright-shop, at the same time, of course, carrying my academic work; I had been successively each year promoted to the next higher class. I not only worked all of that school year in the wheelwrighting-shop, but remained the summer of 1895.

Shortly after the new school year began, my instructor, Mr. M. T. Driver, was selected to take charge of the school's elaborate exhibit at the Cotton States and International Exposition, Atlanta, Ga., at the opening of which Principal Washington had spoken so effectively and powerfully for

THE STORY OF A BLACKSMITH

the Negro people of the country. I had made such substantial progress that Mr. J. H. Washington, then serving as director of mechanical industries, notified me that I had been selected to manage the shop during Mr. Driver's six months' absence.

I was not very much inclined to take the responsibility, but at Tuskegee polite notification of selection to do a thing is a command. I accepted the work and did my very best. There were about twenty young men in the shop when I took charge, some older, some younger than I, but most of whom had been there longer than I had. I had no serious complaints as to the quality of work turned out by me during the instructor's absence.

I now had to my credit more than enough money to carry me through the remaining two years. The next year I entered the day-school. I had become in most respects a new person. I had gone to Tuskegee country-bred, raw, ignorant. The school's transforming influence I was able to note in my carriage, and, of course, in my conversation, in my care for neatness and order, and in the ideals I was forming and trying to live up to. During the summer I returned home for the first time. I worked at my trade during the vacation and earned enough money to buy clothing and other necessaries. I did not return to school until December 28, 1897, as I needed the money I was earning at my trade. I had never earned in money more than the small amounts referred to in the first part of this paper, and so was delighted with my earning capacity.

I then sought work in the blacksmithing-shop, the shop I had first desired to enter, so that I might become a first-class blacksmith in addition to having a working knowledge of wheelwrighting. After completing the school term I went to Montgomery, Ala., and worked as a wheelwright and blacksmith. This outside experience was most helpful to me. My last school year was that of 1899–1900. I was very happy to receive, along with my academic diploma, a certificate also from the blacksmithing division. I was now fitted to begin my life in the great outside world.

My first work was as instructor in blacksmithing and wheelwrighting in the Hungerford Industrial School at Eatonville, Fla. I then secured work at my trades in Birmingham until August, 1901, when three of us who had been classmates at Tuskegee decided to form a partnership and conduct on a large scale a general blacksmithing

THE STORY OF A BLACKSMITH

and wheelwrighting business. I was deputed to select the place where we should locate. After interviewing a number of persons, Anniston, Ala., was suggested, and I decided to go there to personally investigate conditions. After getting there and going about the town, I agreed that at Anniston we should find a place that would properly support our business. There was no place vacant that we could rent, so after some further consideration we decided to purchase a place. This we were fortunate enough to do, and came into possession of a building for our shop, 50 by 60 feet. We met all obligations after opening the shop and secured the most flattering support. Our work met the most exacting requirements, and I was very much disinclined to accept an offer which reached me from Mr. Nathan B. Young, who had had charge of the academic work at Tuskegee during a part of my stay there. Mr. Young, however, represented that I could render much more effective racial service by reaching a large number of persons, young men, daily. After much hesitation I went to the Florida State Normal and Industrial School, to which Mr. Young had been called as President, as instructor in blacksmithing and wheelwrighting, where I have since been employed. I have done well, and am proud that I can say so.

Of my stay at Tuskegee, what shall I say? It was all in all to me. The lessons in shop and class-room, the lessons not at all catalogued that go into character-forming—all of these I found most helpful and invaluable, in making me a man who "thinks and feels." I should be tempted to eulogy should I try to tell how much I owe to Dr. Washington, to his teachers, and to all of the influences that assist the student at Tuskegee.

XIV

A DRUGGIST'S STORY

By David L. Johnston

Shortly after the smoke had cleared away from the battle-fields of the Civil War, I was ushered into the world in a one-room log cabin in Alabama, county of Macon, and near the little town of Tuskegee, afterward made famous by virtue of the fact that there was established near it, by Booker T. Washington, July 4, 1881, the Tuskegee Normal and Industrial Institute. That I have the honor of being an alumnus of that school is one of the best things of which I can boast.

Because I have said that I was born in a one-room log cabin, the reader will readily imagine that my parentage was humble. My mother and father both have gone to the Great Beyond. I bless and revere their memory, for two more noble souls never lived, hampered as they were by slavery and its terrible environments.

My parents continued to live in the one-room

cabin until three other children, making nine in all, had come to them. Another room was added about this time. The biting poverty of it all led my father, with his family, to move to one of the famous cotton plantations of Dallas County, Ala. I seem to recall taking an interest in the world about me quite early. Especially do I recall, as one of my earliest recollections, the death of Garfield, so cruelly slain by the madman Guiteau. My father was greatly distressed, I remember, by his death.

For five successive years my life was spent working each year on the farms for and with my aged father and other members of the family, and spending the time, when not so employed, in near-by public schools, which at that time, as is true in large part now, were conducted only about three months in each year. After having acquired a slight knowledge of mathematics, it was a great pleasure to me to go up each fall to the market at Selma, Ala., with my father, to dispose of the products of the farm. On one occasion there was an apparent interest manifested in me by one of the commission merchants, a white man. He persuaded me to return to Selma, after I had accompanied my father home, and to accept a position

A DRUGGIST'S STORY

with him as office-boy. I returned as agreed, to find either that his promise was a stroke to induce my father to trade with him, or that my stay at home had been too extended—although it was only for three or four days. The position, meanwhile, he said, had been filled by another. Thus, I found myself, a raw country lad, twenty-seven miles from home, without employment and among strangers. Next morning, without the knowledge of my parents, I applied for admittance as a student to the Knox Academy at Selma, and without recommendations, which were immediately demanded of me. I was turned away, but not discouraged, for the next morning, accompanied by a white friend of my father, I again applied and was admitted on his recommendation. An examination entitled me to begin with the fifth-grade class.

I also secured employment at this white man's home. The money thus received paid for my board. By doing odd jobs I managed to make sufficient money to pay for lodging with a good family. I was thus enabled to spend the fall of 1883 and the spring of 1884 in school, to my very great benefit. I was compelled to return home, however, before the term ended, because my father's health completely failed him, to take charge of the farm, as I was the senior male child in the family at that time. My juvenile mind had been awakened by this short school experience in Selma, and from that time forth I had a thirst for more knowledge.

I was absorbed by this longing, but I took up the various other duties which fell to my lot, with the earnest purpose of doing my very best. As a result, with the aid of other members of the family I succeeded in turning over to my invalid father, the succeeding fall, eleven bales of cotton and other farm products in like proportion. My father's health having completely failed, and because of a constantly increasing desire for more knowledge, I conceived the idea of returning to our old home near Tuskegee again.

January, 1885, found us again living in close proximity to the old log cabin in which I was born. Not four years before the Tuskegee Normal and Industrial Institute had been established. The height of my ambition was to be enrolled as a student there, but not having sufficient money to care for the family and remain in school at the same time, and since the term for that year was half spent, I sought employment for the remaining winter months, doing such odd jobs in

A DRUGGIST'S STORY

and around the little town as I could find to do. When spring came, having a fair knowledge of farming, I found ready employment with the planters of that community. With an ambition to enter school the coming fall, I then and there began to study every possible method of economy, and when summer had passed and school-time had come again, with the aid of a younger brother I had cared for the family, and had to my credit my first savings of $85.

Now began the most memorable and the most pleasant days in my life. On the 15th day of September, 1885, I matriculated as a student at Tuskegee, and, after what was then considered a rigid examination, succeeded in entering the Junior class, the lowest class of the normal grade. There was yet before me the task of caring for an aged father and mother. That task I considered a sacred duty, and, with my limited savings in hand, made such purchases as would best give them ordinary comforts through the winter months, and on the 22d day of the same month, after having made such expenditures as I thought necessary, I found that my little pile had been reduced from $85 to $14.50, with which sum I paid my tuition and board at the normal school.

TUSKEGEE AND ITS PEOPLE

I was permitted by the school authorities to work on the school farm the entire term. On the 26th day of May, when the school closed, there yet remained to my credit a sufficient amount to purchase a ticket to Birmingham, and thence out to Pratt City, a near-by suburb. At Pratt City I learned to dig coal, and at the end of every month they paid me in gold. These shining pieces were precious possessions. For four successive summers, in order to get sufficient money to care for my mother and father and make my way in school, I went to Pratt City and worked in the mines, at the furnaces, on the railroads, and around the coke-ovens, enduring hardships which language can hardly describe. But it all paid. The summer of 1888 was a trying one, but when the time came for me to leave for school I had saved $200.

On the 30th day of May, 1889, a new epoch in my life began. I was ushered into the busy world as a graduate of Tuskegee, being in a class of twenty-two. I had looked forward to this event with pride and was very happy.

So imbued was I with the pleasant thought that I was a graduate of Tuskegee, that I little thought of the great responsibilities that awaited me, but when my more sober thought came I

A DRUGGIST'S STORY

realized that I was going from most pleasant surroundings not to return the next year; that I was going out not to return and meet indulgent and persuasive teachers, loving classmates, and devoted friends. I then realized the full meaning of the phrase we had selected that year as our class motto, "Finished, yet just begun." Finished I had at Tuskegee, but I had to begin work and life in the great busy world, with confidence alone as an asset. The Commencement exercises on this particular occasion were most impressive to me, made so in part, I suspect, because I was to be the happy recipient of a coveted diploma. The Commencement speaker was the late Joseph C. Price,[1] of North Carolina, and he was at his best.

Knowing no other field more inviting, I returned to Pratt City, where I had worked successfully. On the 6th of June, 1889, I alighted from the cars, and after spending a few days visiting relatives and friends, applied at No. Four (4) Slope for a set of checks to dig coal. The checks

---

[1] Said to be one of the most eloquent speakers of the Negro people. He died in the prime of life. He was President of Livingston College, which is mainly supported by the African Methodist Episcopal Zion Church, and has a large membership among the colored people.

were readily given me because of my previous record as a miner. After working there during the summer months, and with the same success as had attended me previously, I had secured sufficient money to straighten out my little financial affairs and move my parents and a widowed sister with six small children from Tuskegee to Pratt City, where I had decided permanently to live.

About this time Pratt City was made, by act of the Alabama Legislature, a separate and independent school district, and I had the honor of being elected to the principalship of the Negro school. There I had my first experience as a teacher. I put my whole soul into the work. I had before me the example of the Tuskegee teachers, and the lessons so thoroughly taught there. That I must serve my fellows earnestly and unselfishly was never forgotten.

So pleased was the Board of Education with my work that my salary was soon advanced to $110 per month. This salary was somewhat extraordinary, but Pratt City, Birmingham, Ensley, etc., are in one of the richest mining sections in the world, and the money earned by blacks and whites is greatly in excess of that earned in other parts of the State. I held this position for four years,

A DRUGGIST'S STORY

teaching eight and nine months in the year, and spending the remaining three or four months of the time working in the mines.

After a time my physical system had begun so completely to run down, that I was reluctantly compelled to resign the position of teacher. In the meantime I had purchased a home at Pratt City. Leaving my parents there, I went to Milldale, Ala., to take up new work that offered a change of climate. I returned every fifteen or thirty days, however, to look after the needs of my parents. The entire expense of caring for them, my sister and her children, was quite $60 a month. My work at Milldale made good returns. I was with the Standard Coal Company, and after I had been there fifteen months I had to my credit $1,000, an amount I had long striven to save.

During this time my mother was stricken with fever, and after lingering three months (one of which I spent at her bedside) she died. Our little home was cast in deep sorrow. I returned to Milldale and resumed work there. After two years had expired I had to my credit, I am glad to say, $1,460. With this sum in hand I concluded I would take a course in pharmacy. On October 15, 1894, I entered the Meharry Medical College at Nashville, Tenn., the dean of which is that prince of gentlemen and father of Negro physicians, Dr. George W. Hubbard. I completed the course February 4, 1896, graduating at the head of the class with a general average of $94\frac{1}{4}$ per cent.

I had pleasant associations while there with many of my former Tuskegee class- and schoolmates, among them being Dr. A. H. Kenniebrew, now of Jacksonville, Ill., and for a while Resident Physician of the Tuskegee Institute; Dr. T. N. Harris, of Mobile, Ala., and Dr. A. T. Braxton, of Columbia, Tenn. Each of these is succeeding at the places named most satisfactorily as physicians. At Meharry it was our constant pleasure to refer to our training at Tuskegee, and to acknowledge how indelibly the lessons learned there had been stamped upon our minds and hearts. While there I had the opportunity to compare the instruction received at Tuskegee—that of the academic department—with that of the other institutions of learning in this and even other countries. At Meharry one is thrown in direct contact with educated men and women from the leading Negro colleges of this country, and with many from English institutions of note. After careful investigation I

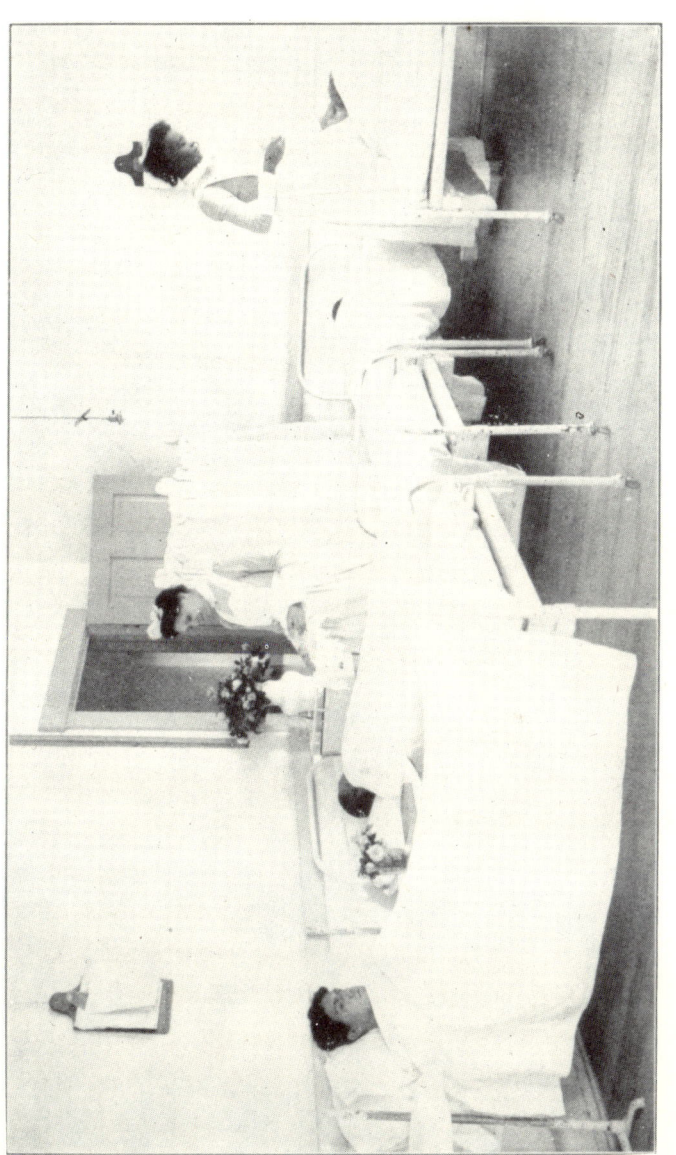

AT THE HOSPITAL.
A corner in the boys' ward.

A DRUGGIST'S STORY

found that the Tuskegee-trained student, at all times, was among the very best there. At Tuskegee I still consider that one of the greatest lessons taught is that of "learning to learn."

At the close of my first year at Meharry I returned to Birmingham, and after a conference with Drs. A. M. Brown and J. B. Kye, colored graduates in medicine and pharmacy, and Mr. George F. Martin, we decided to open a drug-store to be located in Birmingham. About May 7, 1895, the doors of the People's Drug Company were opened to the public, with the above-named gentlemen and myself as the stockholders and owners. Here I invested my first money of consequence in a business enterprise, putting in the greater part of the money to open the business, which invoiced $1,600 or more in about five months after the opening. After affairs were in good running order I left, and returned to Milldale to resume work with the Standard Coal Company. During the spring and summer of that year I realized about $500 from my mining operations.

In the fall of 1895 I returned to Meharry to complete the course already begun. During that fall and winter the business was encouragingly successful under the management of Dr. Kye, aided by Drs. Brown and Mason; for about that time Dr. U. G. Mason, another colored physician, had bought Mr. Martin's interest in the company and had become a partner in the concern. My instructions to the management were to turn over to my father my share of the net proceeds of the business while I was away. My share of the profits kept the family going. My stay at Meharry this last term was most pleasant. I had been promoted to the dignified position of assistant to Dr. W. M. Savier, who was, and is, Dean of the Pharmaceutical Department of the institution.

When I had completed my course I returned to Alabama to begin my work as a pharmacist, and about April 1, 1896, successfully passed the required State examination and was admitted to the practise of pharmacy. I took the examination in Selma, the beautiful little city on the Alabama River where, thirteen years before, I had had my desire for knowledge and better opportunities awakened. I sold my interest in the People's Drug Company at a sacrifice, and immediately opened business on "my own hook" at 34 South Twentieth Street, Birmingham, Ala. In order to begin business with some assurance of success, I organized another company, and had associated with me in

A DRUGGIST'S STORY

this new enterprise (the Union Drug Company) Rev. T. W. Walker, Rev. J. Q. A. Wilhite, and Mr. C. L. Montgomery—all responsible and enterprising citizens of Birmingham.

By hard and diligent work the business proved a success, and from time to time I bought out the interests of the persons named, and accepted as a partner a well-known physician and surgeon, Dr. George H. Wilkerson. Dr. Wilkerson's connection with the business caused it rapidly to increase in volume. When more help was required, as soon it was, we secured the services of Mr. Jimmie James, a young pharmacist who is with me until now. After a period of pleasant business association, Dr. Wilkerson's interests in Mobile, his former home, demanded his presence there. I purchased his interest in the Union Drug Company, and the name was changed to the Union Drug Store. We had but recently located in our own neat little quarters at No. 101 South Twentieth Street, a one-story brick structure, at which place I continued to do business, supported by Drs. W. L. Council and J. B. Goin, who sent their prescriptions to my store, until February 8, 1904. In January, 1904, I secured a lot at No. 601 South Eighteenth Street, Birmingham, and personally erected there a two-story frame building, which I now occupy.

During my short business career since graduation from the medical school, I sought out a partner for life, and was fortunate to win the hand of Miss Pearl L. Strawbridge, of Selma, Ala., who had come to Birmingham to make her home with her brother, Mr. H. Strawbridge, who now holds the honored position of secretary and general manager of one of the largest fraternal insurance concerns in the country owned and controlled by Negroes. Two children, a girl and a boy, have been added to our family since the marriage.

Whatever I have done, or whatever I may do, that will deserve favorable comment, I largely attribute to the fact that I was a student at Tuskegee, and came under the personal care and instruction and guidance of its distinguished Founder and Principal, Dr. Booker T. Washington, and that I have striven, from the first day until now, to put into practise the lessons taught me by him and his excellent body of teachers. At Tuskegee we were taught the truism, " If you can not find a way, make one." I hope I am not immodest in saying that I think I have, in some degree, done this.

XV

THE STORY OF A SUPERVISOR OF MECHANICAL INDUSTRIES

By James M. Canty

I was born December 23, 1863, in Marietta, Cobb County, Ga. My parents, James and Adella Canty, were slaves. I am the eldest of two brothers and three sisters, who are all living. My father died in the fall of 1895. Since that time, because of circumstances and inclinations, it has been my lot to look after the welfare of my mother, who is still living in Marietta, Ga., a place of about four thousand inhabitants.

At an early age I entered the public school at my home. My father, however, soon put me to work, so that I grew up quite ignorant of books. He was a carpenter and butcher, and fairly skilled in working iron. For a number of years he kept a meat-market. At the age of sixteen I was doing the principal part of the butchering. Some years later, when father was appointed street "boss" of the town, I worked as one of the street laborers. When he changed his occupation from street "boss" to farmer, mine likewise changed. The rule was, a change from one occupation to another, working day by day without attention to mental growth, and having no thought of the future, till I was persuaded to join several other boys who had decided to form themselves into a night-class for purposes of self-improvement.

About this time, in compliance with my father's desire, and to my delight, I entered a carriage factory as an apprentice. It was while working there that I received a newspaper from a girl student at Tuskegee Normal and Industrial Institute. The paper contained a long descriptive article, with cuts of buildings, class-rooms, teachers, and students. The student who had sent the paper was from my home, and with it came a letter from her stating that she had spoken to Mr. Washington in my interest, and that if I would come to Tuskegee I would be given a chance to get an education. I shall never forget the impression made upon my mind by that newspaper article and the young woman's letter.

My father was consulted, and advised against my going away to school, saying: "You can continue night-school here at home and at the same time learn a trade. I never went to school a day

IN THE TIN-SHOP.

THE STORY OF A SUPERVISOR

in my life." Well, I knew that my father, nevertheless, could read and write a little and do some figuring, and that he at one time came within a few votes of being elected to the State Legislature of Georgia. Contrary to his advice, I concluded to go to Tuskegee. Looking back now, and connecting the present with the day on which my decision was made, I think that time and events have vindicated the wisdom of my decision.

After giving my employer two weeks' notice of my intention to give up my work, I hastened to arrange my affairs, fearing that procrastination might allow some event to change my mind and thus alter the whole course of my life. Two weeks after giving notice to my employer, I started for Tuskegee. I bought a ticket to Atlanta, where I spent the night. The next morning I went to the station and asked for a ticket to Tuskegee. The agent, on looking over his guide-books, said to me: "There is no such place as Tuskegee in the guide-books." I walked away from the window, thinking that, after all, Tuskegee was some place that existed only on paper.

Not wishing to give it up, I turned and approached the agent again. He got out maps and guides, and finally found Tuskegee, but said he could not sell me a ticket to that place as it was not on a railroad, and that the best thing for me to do was to purchase a ticket to Chehaw, Ala. So my ticket read, From Atlanta to Chehaw. On turning to leave the ticket-agent, I inquired how I could get to Tuskegee from Chehaw. He replied that he did not know. But I got there, going from Chehaw over a narrow-gauge road. The engine that pulled the one coach composing the train was named the "Klu-Klux," a thing I had heard of but had not understood. That there should be many new things to me in the world was not to be wondered at, when it was known that I had never before been out of the county in which I was born except on three occasions, when my trips extended only to adjoining counties.

It was in the month of March, 1886, while passing through the town of Tuskegee, that I beheld for the first time, standing at a distance, the institution that has, in my opinion, done more than any other one agency to elevate the Negroes of the South. About eight o'clock P.M. I arrived on the campus and was assigned to a room by the commandant, through the officer of the day.[1]

---

[1] The West Point system is followed in training the young men. Except that there are no guns, a complete battalion organization exists.

THE STORY OF A SUPERVISOR

For about thirty minutes I was alone in the room, the student body being at devotional exercises— the Tuskegee Institute holding its daily devotions at night, instead of in the morning like most schools. This is done on account of the day- and night-school system, it being impossible to get all the students of the school together except at night after the night-school session.

While sitting and thinking of home, of the past, and of the future, I took out my pocketbook and counted $7.50. Not one cent more had I, and as I looked at the money with the thought that $7.50 represented the entire savings of my life up to that time, gloom and despondency almost overcame me.

The next morning I went to the Principal's office. From there I went to be examined, and then again to see the Principal. Mr. Washington explained that board was charged for at $8 per month, and that my books would be sold to me at cost. He informed me further that if I entered night-school I would be able to work out my board and accumulate each month a balance to be used in paying my expenses when I entered day-school. I was made to understand that this offer was on condition that my work and conduct be in every way satisfactory. As the amount of money I had did not justify me in entering day-school, I matriculated as a night-school student. The blacksmith-shop being short of students, I was assigned to this division of industry.

During the remaining part of the year, and the following summer, I worked in the shop ten hours each day, except Sundays, and devoted about two hours and a half at night to study and recitations. It is no easy task, during warm weather in Alabama, for one to work ten hours a day and spend two and a half hours at night studying in a room lighted by several large lamps suspended from the ceiling. Yet this is what hundreds of poor boys and girls have done at Tuskegee. Hundreds still attend the night-school, but electric lights have taken the place of the large oil-lamps. Tuskegee is now more modern than it was when I was a student there. Barrels and boxes are no longer used in the raw state for furniture, as was largely the case at that time. Day-students were required to work one school-day each week and every other Saturday. I was a student nearly five years, counting the time when I was a night-student.

After I entered day-school it was necessary that I should work not only on my regular work-

THE STORY OF A SUPERVISOR

days and two Saturdays each month, but whenever there was work to be done and I could find time in which to do it. During my entire life at Tuskegee I worked every Saturday except three.

I was not long at Tuskegee before an indescribable force began to have its influence upon me. Whatever this power may be called, it was both refining and energizing. People who know the school and have been there and know of its influence, call this force " the Tuskegee spirit." This spirit, to the student possessing a spark of manhood, is irresistible. The change in a student at Tuskegee is not sudden, nor is it wrought by any one element. Things that may seem small when taken separately, are invaluable when considered in the aggregate.

At Tuskegee one's attention is constantly called to little things. It was a habit of mine, I regret to say, to give little or no thought to my hat being on my head when I was in any of the boys' dormitories, or when passing through the halls of the buildings containing the class-rooms. My attention was finally called to this habit by one of the lady teachers. Passing me one day in the hall, she said: " Canty, you have a habit of wearing your hat through the halls. It is a very bad habit." When I entered Tuskegee I had not worn a night-shirt since I was a child. Here it was soon impressed upon me that sleeping in a night-shirt was a sign of cleanliness, of civilization. If there is any place where cleanliness is regarded and practised as one of God's first laws, that place is Tuskegee.

One day Mr. Washington sent for me to come to his office. I received the message with fear and trembling. I had, before this time, had but one opportunity to speak to Mr. Washington, and then only for a few minutes upon the day following my arrival. On my way to the office I wondered if any rule of the institution had been violated by me. Though I had been there only three or four weeks, I knew a request for a student to report at the Principal's office meant that he was to be given notice of imminent punishment, or consulted upon some matter of vital interest.

When I entered the office, Mr. Washington asked me to write to two or three worthy young men at my home and inquire if they desired a chance to work their way through school. Several days had passed when I received an answer from one of the young men to whom I wrote. It so hap-

THE STORY OF A SUPERVISOR

pened that on the day the letter was received I met Mr. Washington on his way to his office, and said, "Mr. Washington [drawing the letter from my pocket], I have received a letter from—" Here my first sentence was cut short by Mr. Washington forcibly gesticulating and saying, "Come to the office; come to the office and see me there." That one lecture on business methods impressed me in a way that a chapter of this length could not have done.

One day I closed a door with considerable force, which attracted the attention of one of the teachers. The teacher, in my presence, again opened the door and gently closed it, noiselessly and without a word. I have never since forgotten the proper way in which to open and close doors. Little details are big essentials in the rounding out of character. They show the influence of the "Tuskegee spirit." But, after all, this spirit would not be so irresistible in its influence for good if the teachers and officers of the institution were not the embodiment and living example of it. Here, as elsewhere and everywhere, example is more potent than precept.

Every institution has policies peculiarly its own. It is necessary that every teacher and officer support that policy to make it effective. Each instructor has a distinct individuality that becomes a part of the student, in smaller or greater degree, and at the same time gives force and strength to the policies of the institution. Though I felt the influence of every one of the thirty-odd teachers then at Tuskegee, the individuality of some of these made a very great impression on me. I remember Mr. W. D. Wilson as a very quiet and effective disciplinarian. Mr. Warren Logan, the treasurer, has the ability to teach the student the value of a dollar by making him sacrifice almost beyond the point of endurance. At the same time, with a smile and a cheerful disposition, he would make the student feel that his burden was light. Through the kindness and special interest manifested in me by Mr. M. T. Driver, who was in charge of wheelwrighting and blacksmithing, I made rapid progress at my trade. Miss Adella H. Hunt, who has since become the wife of Treasurer Logan, was then a teacher who had the faculty of touching a responsive chord in a student. Mrs. Booker T. Washington, then Miss Margaret J. Murray, impressed me very much. Strong and resourceful in dealing with students, she always won the best that was in them. My

STUDENTS CANNING FRUIT.

THE STORY OF A SUPERVISOR

student-days were almost at an end when she came to Tuskegee.

I shall ever feel grateful to Mr. J. H. Washington for the encouragement he gave me. Being superintendent of industries, he was then, as he is now, in constant touch with every male student. He is a believer in, and a firm advocate of, steady, thorough, earnest work, and is quick to see, appreciate, and encourage the smallest degree of ability shown by any student. No time seemed too valuable for him to give in trying to advance a student in his work. I might add here that the teachers here named are, with two exceptions, among the pioneers in the building of the school.

Mr. Booker T. Washington's personality is the great thing at Tuskegee, and every student who goes there feels the strength of the man's rugged individuality. "Mr. B. T." is an affectionate term used by the students, but it springs from an indescribable, spontaneous feeling of love and veneration. His Sunday evening talks to the students are to me like the Book of Proverbs, always timely, encouraging, and applicable to the affairs of every-day life. It is from these family talks that the students learn, as they never have before, the beauty that lies in real, every-day Christianity, and in living a real and simple life. It is from these talks that the students learn so much of the great heart and center of the institution. Mr. Washington still delivers Sunday evening talks when at school, and they are published in the school's weekly paper, The Tuskegee Student. Graduates throughout the country eagerly read these talks with the same interest and pleasure with which they listened to them while in school.

Mr. Washington taught then, as he teaches now, psychology to the Senior class. The student has not become intimately acquainted with Mr. Washington until he becomes a Senior. It is here that the members of the Senior class talk of their past and future lives and receive the outpourings of a great but simple soul. Mr. Washington's long and frequent absences from the school are no less regretted by the teachers than by the students.

Soon after entering school I began to think of what I should do after graduating. My inclination led me to feel that success would be found along mercantile lines. In spite of this I applied myself zealously to my trade. During my last two years in school I did what teaching in blacksmithing my literary work permitted, the school being without an instructor in this industry for a short

THE STORY OF A SUPERVISOR

while. There was then no course in engineering or in machinery, so I did all the pipe-work and kept the machinery of the school in repair. In this way I learned something of machinery without an instructor. With some pride I recall the fact that I "ironed" the first farm-wagons, the first two-seated spring-wagon, and the first buggy made at Tuskegee. I also "piped" the school's first bathroom for girls.

In May of my Senior year I was very much surprised to receive a note from Principal Booker T. Washington intimating that he desired me to connect myself with the school the following year. Later he stated the nature of the work he wanted me to do. I accepted the offer he made me. I was asked to teach in the night-school and instruct in the blacksmith-shop one-half of each week-day.

A few days after graduation I visited my home with the intention of spending the summer there. I was there about three weeks, when I received a letter from Mr. John H. Washington requesting my return to Tuskegee the next week, if I could so arrange. He at that time was both superintendent of industries and commandant. On my return he informed me that the Principal had decided that since his duties as superintendent of industries were so important, he was to be relieved of all others, and that in lieu of instructing in the blacksmith-shop, I was to be offered the work as commandant.

At once I set about getting the boys' rooms in order for the opening of school. During the two previous years, even while a student, I had virtually been acting as commandant, since no one man could carry double responsibilities such as Mr. J. H. Washington had been carrying. I was appointed commandant, and placed in charge of the night-school for a year. I then resigned, looking forward to following my old-time inclination of engaging in some mercantile business. I knew that I could accumulate means for this purpose sooner by working at my trade, as I received two dollars per day working as a blacksmith during vacation seasons at Birmingham, Ala.

My first marriage occurred in 1891, my wife being Miss Sarah J. Harris. We were classmates at Tuskegee four years, and graduated together. She died in 1894 at Institute, W. Va. Our long association and acquaintance made us understand each other even before we were married. Having become a Christian before myself, she had much to do with my conversion while I was a student. She

THE STORY OF A SUPERVISOR

was a great help to me in many ways, and through her economy I was able to begin the purchase of my first property. Portia, the oldest and only child now living of the three children born to us, is in the Little Girls' Home at Knoxville College, Tenn. In 1897 I was married to Miss Florence Lovett, a graduate of Storer College, Harpers Ferry, W. Va. She shares my burdens, and is in every way a part of whatever success I am able to achieve. Four children have been born to us.

After resigning my position as commandant and head of the night-school at Tuskegee, I spent a few weeks visiting relatives, and then returned to Marietta. Here I worked at my trade in a carriage-shop, where a great deal of machine-work was done for two furniture factories and a planing-mill. Much of my time was spent in repairing machinery and making bits and knives for the factories.

While at home I tried to make myself a part of the people in a helpful way. I lived with my parents about two miles from the town. On my father's farm was a church, the ground for which had been given by my father. I was elected superintendent of the Sunday-school of this church, and filled this position as long as I remained there. Soon after the Sunday-school was started it occurred to me that the young people of the community could be greatly helped by a literary society. With the aid of others I organized a society and was elected its president. We met every Friday night at the house of some member. It was the custom to meet at different places, so that the long distances necessary to walk would be equally shared by all. Even by this arrangement some had to walk three and four miles, but the pleasure and benefit derived from attending the society repaid us for the trouble.

After I had been at my home about a year, I received a letter from Mr. Booker T. Washington requesting that I write to Mr. J. Edwin Campbell, Principal of the West Virginia Colored Institute, then located near Farm, W. Va. Enclosed with Mr. Washington's letter was one Mr. Campbell had written, asking that a Tuskegee graduate be named to take the position of Superintendent of Mechanics. This title has since been changed to Superintendent of Mechanical Industries. On January 3, 1893, I arrived at the West Virginia Colored Institute and entered upon my duties, and have held the position ever since.

STARTING A NEW BUILDING.
Student masons laying the foundation in brick.

THE STORY OF A SUPERVISOR

In the early summer of 1898 Mr. J. H. Hill, who was then principal, resigned to accept a Lieutenancy in a company of United States Volunteers. During the interim following the resignation of Mr. Hill and the appointment of Mr. J. McHenry Jones, the present principal, I was placed in charge of the school by the Board of Regents. Mr. Jones was elected principal September 21, 1898.

Until the fall of 1898 my duties were many and varied, as I had no assistance in carrying on the industrial work of the school. I taught blacksmithing, carpentering, and mechanical drawing. Besides this, I have had to put the sewerage system into the institution, and the heating apparatus into several of the school buildings. Still, a part of my time in 1894 was devoted to teaching in the literary department. My work now, while as exacting as ever, is more along the line of superintending the mechanical industries and in teaching mechanical drawing.

The school has grown, since my coming here, from 3 teachers and 30 students to a faculty of 18 teachers and 187 students. There are 6 instructors in the mechanical department for boys. We give instruction in carpentry, printing, blacksmithing, brick masonry, plastering, wheelwrighting, and mechanical drawing. These industries are housed in a building—the " A. B. White Trades Building"—that cost $35,000.

In concluding this sketch, I repeat with emphasis what I said in the beginning: Whatever my accomplishments may be, the credit is due to Tuskegee. I do not wish in life to be regarded as a man of chance possibilities, but rather as one who has consistently persevered in all of his struggles. Tuskegee teaches nothing with greater force than that success lies in that direction. Principal Washington, among other things, has taught that it is necessary to get property and have a bank-account. I have complied with that teaching. I own a farm of 100 acres within one-eighth of a mile of the school. My first property, which I still own, consists of a one-acre lot and a seven-room house. It gives me pleasure to contribute annually $10 to Tuskegee, although this but inadequately expresses my gratitude to the institution to which I owe so much.

XVI

A NEGRO COMMUNITY BUILDER

By Russell C. Calhoun

I HAVE been asked to here set forth incidents of my life as I remember them, especially as they relate to my life at Tuskegee and my work since leaving there. Though there have been quite a number of events in my life, it is somewhat difficult for me to give them in the way they are now desired, as it never occurred to me that they would be worth repeating.

Concerning my ancestry, it is impossible for me to give anything beyond my maternal grandfather, who was about three-fourths Indian. My recollections of him go back to the time when I was about six or seven years of age. My mother, having more children than she could really care for, decided to allow one of my brothers, who was perhaps a year and a half younger than I, and myself, to live with him and his second wife.

My grandfather was quite seventy-five years of age when we went to live with him, and was too feeble to work. He was supported from the poorhouse, which gave him a peck of meal, $2\frac{1}{2}$ pounds of bacon, 1 pound of coffee, 1 pound of brown sugar, and once a month 25 cents' worth of flour. That, together with the little his wife could earn from place to place, constituted the "rations" of all of us for a week.

Of my birth no record was kept, my mother having been a slave. All I have been able to learn of the date of my birth is what my mother remembers connected with the close of slavery. In trying to ascertain from her when I was born, she said, "You was born some time just after Christmas, in the month of January, the third year after the surrender."

My mother had twelve children. I was the eighth child and the second one born after slavery. All except two of the children were born in the same one-room log cabin with a dirt floor, in the town of Paulding, Jasper County, Miss. My mother did the cooking for her master's family and the plantation help, did all of the milking, and was also washer-woman.

In the summer of 1896 I again visited Paulding, just after graduating from Tuskegee. I had to go there to move my aged mother to more

A NEGRO COMMUNITY BUILDER

comfortable quarters. She was quite ill, and died soon after I reached Florida with her. When I went to Paulding I measured the house in which I was born, and found it to be 9 feet wide, 17 feet long, 7 feet high, with no windows, with but one door, and a dirt chimney. The furnishing as I remember it was composed of a chair, a stool, a table, and my mother's bed, which was constructed in one corner of the house. The bed was made by putting a post in the ground and nailing two pieces of wood to the wall from this post, then by putting in a floor, making something like a box to hold the bedding. The children slept in a similarly constructed place, except that the mattress was on the ground and was filled with straw. Our bedding, for the most part, was what wearing apparel we possessed thrown over us at night. Outside the house was a long bench, which was kept for the accommodation of visitors.

A peculiar incident in our home life happened one Sunday morning in March—one Easter Sunday. All of the smaller children were seated on the floor eating their breakfasts from pans and skillets, when a big black snake, without any regard for the children, went into a hole by the fireplace. When one of my older brothers undertook to find him and opened this hole, he found, instead of one, four black snakes that had been wintering in the side of the house.

There was no church or school for us in that whole section. A white man, a Doctor Cotton, to whom I was afterward given until I should become twenty-one years of age, sent his boys to a school which required that they walk eight miles to it and return each day.

When I was perhaps eight years of age I remember that my mother and all of the children went to Spring Hill to a camp-meeting; that was the first service at which I had heard a minister. They had a Sunday-school, and I was put into a class. The teacher gave us leaflets and asked us to read where we found the big letter "A." This was the first and only letter that I knew for many years. This camp-meeting was held once a year, though at times there would be prayer-meetings among the different families on the plantation.

My mother, being a hard-working woman and knowing the value of keeping children busy, compelled every one of us to work in some way around the house or on the farm. I know of no lesson which she taught me and which has been of more value to me than that of " doing with your might what your hands find to do." It was a rule of her household that we should not go to bed without having water in the house. The water had to be brought from a spring a mile and a half away. I remember clearly how one night one of my brothers and myself tried to deceive her; how we secured some not overclear water from a hole near-by our home, and how she pitched it out and sent us the whole distance to the spring. Although this was many years ago, I now see, more and more, what it means to go all the way to the real spring, and I thank her memory for the lesson.

When I was about ten years of age the same Doctor Cotton of whom I have spoken came to my grandmother's to hire one of the boys to mind the bars, as the teams were hauling corn to the barn and the drivers did not want to put them up each time. I was delighted to be the chosen one of the two. My first chance to earn money was thus offered.

I stayed there every day from sunrise to sunset for a little more than three weeks, and it was a happy day when Doctor Cotton requested all hands to come up and be paid off. I do not know what the rest received; though I had boarded from the scanty fare before mentioned at my grandmother's home, he gave me fifteen cents, paying me in three nickels. I had never had any money in my hands before, and for fear I might lose it I put it in my pocket and held the pocket with both hands, and ran for more than two miles, carrying it home. One nickel of the three was given me for my share.

Seemingly this Doctor Cotton was very much impressed with the way I had performed my duty at the bars, for in the next few weeks he again visited my grandmother. I was quite anxious to know what his frequent visits meant, and was very much delighted, as well as surprised, when it was told me, one morning when it was very cold, and I had on only two pieces of clothing made of some very coarse material resembling canvas, that I was to live with Doctor Cotton until reaching manhood, and was to eat at his house. He told me in my grandmother's presence that if I would stay with him until I was twenty-one years of age I would receive a horse, a bridle and saddle, a suit of clothes, and $10, in addition to my "keep." This was such an apparently big offer that my grandmother's and my heart leaped for joy.

When I had lived with him for a few days I had given me the first pair of shoes, of the copper-toe variety, I ever wore.

A NEGRO COMMUNITY BUILDER

I have never forgotten my first day's stay at this new home. My whole object that first day was to eat everything in sight. At my own home I slept on the dirt floor; at this new home I slept in the attic, my bed being a pile of cotton-seed with a quilt for covering. My duty at this new home was to attend to the horses, to bring the cows from the pasture, sweep the yard, wait on the table, nurse two children, etc. I stayed at this place for two and one-half years, and as my knowledge of things increased my duties became more and more exacting.

During this whole time, and for two years before, I had not seen or heard from my mother. I was twenty miles from any railroad, and had never seen or heard of a railroad train. We lived on the public road between Paulding and Enterprise, and by some means I heard that my mother had gone to the " railroad." Though I had never been away on my own resources, I resolved to do better than I was doing. I remember very well that it was Monday morning when one of the doctor's daughters said to me, " Russell, you go down to 'Vina's house, tell her to come and scour for me; come by the store and get a package of soda; then come through the field and drive the turkeys home." Providence never favored any one more than it did me on that day. I went by the store and told them to do up the soda, I went by and told 'Vina that she was wanted, but I did not drive the turkeys home.

I started out in search of my mother, and after walking more than half the distance I overtook an ox-team, and the driver allowed me to ride a part of the way. I reached the railroad town about night, and standing there was a freight train of the Mobile and Ohio Railroad.

I was never so frightened in all my life as when the whistle blew and this object moved away. I remember asking the driver of the ox-team where the thing's eyes were, and where the horses were that pulled it.

The doctor, suspecting that I had gone to Enterprise in search of my mother, made plans to capture me and have me returned, but all of this failed. By good fortune I found my brother, who was married and living in this town; here again I became a nurse, having to care for his two children.

Afterward I went to live with a white family which was very kind to me. The young man who carried me to his house as a nurse put into my hands, after I had been there some months, the first spelling-book I had ever had; saying to me that if I would stay with them for two years, he would at the end of that time send me to school. I stayed at this place for some months, when my mother came from somewhere, I know not where, and with five of the boys we joined ourselves together to work on a plantation on "halves." We worked very hard that year.

Our food was furnished by the owner of the plantation. On many of those long, cold days, for all day, we had only a "pone" of corn bread. At the close of the year, after the owner had taken his half, and on account of bad management on the part of an older brother who had charge of affairs, my mother and her younger children received nothing for the year's work, and this, notwithstanding the fact that we made five and one-half bales of cotton and a large quantity of corn and peas. I received as my "salary" for the year's work one shirt worth thirty cents and a pair of suspenders worth about fifteen cents. I resolved to run away again. This trip was made at night, on foot, over newly laid railroad-ties, for a distance of seventeen miles.

I reached Meridian, Miss., at a late hour of the night, and took refuge in a shed used for the storing of railroad iron. The next morning I overheard two colored men, who were on their way to get meat ready for the town-market two miles away, talking. I joined these men, and sought employment along with them, but they soon learned that I knew nothing of "butchering." However, the owner of the pen, who had a large garden, gave me a trial, and I remained with him for three years.

After I was there a little more than a year my work was to plant and care for the small seeds. This man, Mr. Nady Sims, was a good man, and I had no cause for leaving him except that of wishing to get a place to earn more money, that I might help care for my mother and her smaller children.

I went next to a brick-yard, where I received fifty cents per day. There were three boys at each "table," and we had to "off-bear" 5,500 bricks, the task for each day. This was indeed hard work.

Drifting into hotel work, I soon acquired the habit of most of those who are engaged in such work: I spent all I earned for fine clothes.

During my stay on the vegetable farm I boarded at the home of one of the young men previously referred to, whose sister, Mary Clinton, who has since become my wife and devoted as-

A NEGRO COMMUNITY BUILDER

sistant, one day heard a woman say she knew of a school in Alabama where boys and girls could work for their education, and that she was going to send her boy to that school. This thought remained in her mind for some months, and she decided to go to Tuskegee, though her brothers and sisters discouraged the idea, feeling, as they said, that if she went to this unknown place her whole life would be a failure.

She reached Tuskegee in September, 1885, at a time when there was but one building. She worked in many places while there, including the laundry, the teachers' dining-room, the sewing division, with Principal Washington's family, as well as with the families of other teachers. On account of poor health, especially because of throat trouble, she was compelled to return home at the end of five years without graduating.

No sooner had she reached home again than she began a crusade for Tuskegee. I was then twenty-one years of age, had never had a day's schooling, and could read but very little. I proposed marriage to Miss Clinton as soon as she returned, but she replied: " You do not know anything except about hotel work. I have been to Tuskegee and see the need of your knowing something. I also need to know more than I do. I can easily marry some one who knows more than you do, but if you will go to school I will assist you in any way that I can." This proposition I accepted, and on September 2, 1890, I reached Tuskegee and began my first day in school.

I had some knowledge of carpentry, and was for that reason assigned to the carpenter-shop for work during the day; I attended school at night.

There were ninety-three young men and women in the class when I entered school; of that number only two, in addition to myself, remained through the entire course. I can never forget my examination by Miss Maggie J. Murray, now Mrs. Booker T. Washington. There were quite three hundred new students in the chapel of Porter Hall, one of the oldest buildings of the institution, taking examinations at the same time.

She gave me two slips of paper, a pencil, and the questions, and said to me: "Write the answers to these questions." She went about other duties, and after about three hours returned to me for my papers; then for the first time in my life I learned the meaning of geography and arithmetic. The slips of paper mentioned asked

A NEGRO COMMUNITY BUILDER

questions on those subjects. I had not put anything on the paper. She asked me if I knew of any large cities; if I had ever crossed a river or seen a hill; if I knew the name of the railroad over which I had come to reach Tuskegee.

I was able to answer each of these questions very readily; and she said, " Calhoun, that is geography."

She assigned me to one of the lowest classes in the night-school. I bought books which cost $1.70, and had fifty-two cents left. I soon spent the fifty cents.

For seven months during my first year's stay my only possession was represented by a two-cent stamp. I had had many " good friends " before going to Tuskegee, and debated long as to which of them I should devote the two-cent stamp, trusting to receive some financial aid. Finally I decided on one of these " good friends." I used the stamp, and have not heard from him from that day to this.

While carpentry was my special trade, I found the opportunity to get information as to the other industries on the grounds. All of this supplemental study has proved most helpful to me in my present work.

TUSKEGEE AND ITS PEOPLE

Most persons who enter school for the first time, and especially industrial schools, get wrong impressions at the start. Notwithstanding the fact that I was a young man who had "knocked about" the world quite a little, I thought I had made a mistake in entering school, and did not begin to see that I had done properly until I had been there for eight or nine months. I asked for an excuse to leave school early in the first term; it was denied me. I tried to sell my trunk for $7, so that I might run away. I had a penchant for running away from disagreeable surroundings. I was offered $6, but for the sake of the difference of $1 I decided to remain.

I do not hesitate to say that each day I live in my heart I most heartily thank the good friends who have made it possible for Tuskegee to be; I am also most grateful that I was able to reach it and receive the training which I received there. I did nothing great while at Tuskegee, but I remember with pride that I gave no trouble in any way during my sojourn.

I used my spare hours making picture-frames, repairing window-shades, making flower-stands and flower-boxes, and working flower-gardens for the various Faculty families. The money received

A NEGRO COMMUNITY BUILDER

I saved until the end of the school term. At the end of each term there were always a large number of students who cared nothing for their books, and all but gave them away. Looking three months ahead, I bought these books and sold them to new students who entered the following year.

One year alone I cleared $40 in this way. The second-hand book business among the students began from this effort on my part to add to my little pile of cash money.

Having completed the course with a class of thirty-one members, May 26, 1896, I started straight for my home, Meridian, Miss.

For six years, as a student, I had been at Tuskegee and under its influences; now I had only my conscience to dictate to me and to keep me straight. Feeling that I could not do much good at Meridian, I started for Texas, having had a position promised me.

I reached Mobile, Ala., while en route, and heard that Miss Mary Clinton, previously mentioned, was in Tampa, Fla. Feeling that she still had some interest in me, I again decided to go to her for advice.

I reached the city of Tampa with but a small sum in my pocket. The town was undergoing a "boom," and I was certain that it would not be long before I would be earning something, but, to my disappointment, I found about thirty men looking for every job in sight. After much wearying search I became thoroughly convinced that Tampa was too large a city not to give me something to do besides "looking up into the air." Finally, one rainy morning I secured work at a freight-house.

It was my lot to go first up the wet, steep, and slippery gang-plank. Not being used to such a task, I fell, the truck with 350 pounds narrowly escaping me. I got up and made a second attempt to carry my load, and with success. I had been there two months when the agent wanted some new shelves built in the storehouse. He told one of his employees to go for a carpenter. He replied, "This man Calhoun can do any such work you want done." The agent had me get my tools and do the work. A few days afterward he wanted a first-class cook to prepare and serve a special Christmas dinner. The same employee told him, "Calhoun can do it."

The motto of my class was, "We Conquer by Labor."

On April 29, 1897, both Miss Clinton and

A NEGRO COMMUNITY BUILDER

myself were called to a school in South Carolina, and in a simple way, with $50 saved, we married and boarded the train for our new field of labor. After giving up our work and reaching Sanford, 125 miles away, we received a letter asking us to defer our coming until the following October.

This was a very, very sad disappointment and trial to us. It was two weeks before the State examinations would be held. We prepared as best we could, and as a result of the examination we were sent to Eatonville, Fla., to take charge of the public school there. Eatonville is a Negro town with colored officers, a colored postmaster, and colored merchants. There is not a single white person living within the incorporated city; it promises to be a unique community. It is situated near the center of Orange county, six miles from Orlando, the county seat, and is two miles from the Seaboard Air-Line Railroad, and one and one-half miles from the Atlantic Coast Line Railroad.

It was said by the late Bishop H. B. Whipple, of Wisconsin—whose winter home for a number of years was a half mile from this place—who had helped the people of this community, and who was a constant helper and adviser to my wife and me in our work until his death, that you might travel the whole State over and not find a more healthy place. We were here but a few days when we decided that this was the place for us to begin putting into practise the lessons taught us at Tuskegee. We felt that we wanted to do something toward helping our people. We decided to cast our lot permanently at Eatonville.

Our first "industrial" service was done with the aid of the school children: we cleaned the street of tin cans and other rubbish.

We found the lessons in economy which we had received at Tuskegee very valuable to us at this trying time. We felt that if we would properly impress the lessons most needed we should own a home, a cow, some chickens, a horse, and a garden; we felt that there should be tangible ownership on the part of the people of some of these things, at any rate.

These things we started to get as soon as possible. We wanted to teach the people by example.

After talking in a general way for some days of the value of industrial education, coupled with that of intelligent class-room instruction, Mrs. Calhoun succeeded in getting four girls to come to her home for sewing lessons. That was the first step.

A NEGRO COMMUNITY BUILDER

Incidentally, we heard of the philanthropic instincts of a gentleman, Mr. E. C. Hungerford, living at Chester, Conn., who had conditionally offered to another school twenty acres of land, and whose offer was not met. I wrote to him asking if he would give us the land. He replied that he would be glad to give us forty acres if we would use it for school purposes.

On February 24, 1899, having the deed in hand, a board of trustees was selected, and, with the aid of nine men who cleared one and one-half acres of land while their wives furnished the dinner, we started what is now the Robert C. Hungerford Industrial School. The new school now owns 280 acres of land secured as follows: From Mr. and Mrs. E. C. Hungerford, 160 acres; from Mr. and Mrs. T. W. Cleavland, 40 acres; from Mrs. Nancy B. Hungerford, 40 acres; by purchase, an additional 40 acres.

The school has two dormitories, Booker T. Washington Hall, the J. W. Alfred Cluett Memorial Hall, and six other buildings used for shops, barn, and dining-room. The total value of the property, clear of all indebtedness, is $22,445. We teach the boys blacksmithing, wheelwrighting, carpentry, agriculture, stock-raising, poultry-raising, and truck-gardening; the girls receive instruction in dressmaking, plain sewing, cooking, laundering, millinery, basketry, and housekeeping. We give no industry at the expense of the literary work.

The academic department covers a useful course of the English branches. The moral, religious, industrial, and financial influence of the school upon the community, as well as upon the students who have attended, who come from many counties in the State, has grown steadily as the years have come and gone. The school has at present forty-five young people in the boarding department, including seven teachers, three of whom have come from Tuskegee; a large enrolment of students from the immediate community and from the surrounding territory.

I have not said very much regarding the difficulties, the struggles, to plant this work, but I am glad to say that from the beginning we have had the friendliest support and advice from all the white people of this section, officials and citizens alike.

I owe much of my success in the work here to the cheerful and freely given counsel at all times of Hon. W. L. Palmer, Representative in the

A NEGRO COMMUNITY BUILDER

State Legislature, and to the members of the Board of Public Instruction of this (Orange) county.

The colored people have had little to give in cash, but have been most liberal in their contributions of labor. They have been willing to help themselves.

My constant, my most earnest desire is to prove myself worthy of my opportunities, that I may continue to be a worthy representative of Tuskegee. I feel that I owe all that I am, all that I can hope to be, to the training of my mother, to the constant help and counsel of my wife, and to Tuskegee, my Tuskegee, from which I have received so many lessons that have been of incalculable help to me. I look back to my lessons in carpentry, as well as to all the others, with gratitude for the thoroughness insisted upon in all directions. I was rescued from a life of aimlessness, and put in the way of doing something of good for my fellows.

XVII

THE EVOLUTION OF A SHOE-MAKER

By Charles L. Marshall

I was born in the town of Henderson, State of Kentucky, January 1, 1867. My father and mother were both slaves. My father rendered service during the Civil War as a Union soldier.

As early as I can remember there was in Henderson a public free school for colored children. In 1872 there came to our town a young man from Louisville, Ky., John K. Mason by name, to take charge of the school. How he secured his education I never learned, but that he devoted his life to the uplift of his race is everywhere in that section clearly in evidence. Unfortunately, I was not permitted as a boy to go to school, but became a factory lad instead; for, almost before I was old enough to begin my education, I was put to work in a tobacco factory, and there I remained. From childhood to manhood I think I spent, all told, not more than three years in school.

EVOLUTION OF A SHOEMAKER

Somehow I had a faint idea of the value of education, and manifested a desire for learning by securing the services of a young man, whose country-school term had expired, to give me lessons at night when not otherwise engaged. He was quite a "society" man, so that my school-nights were few in number.

While my father did not provide for my education, he was himself an industrious man and provided that I should not be idle. Each year, when the tobacco season was over, I had regular employment in a cooper-shop with my father, and I learned to make barrels and hogsheads. This trade I found to be quite valuable, for before I was twenty-one years of age I was able to demand wages of two dollars a day as a cooper.

Quite incidentally I heard of the work being done at Tuskegee by Principal Booker T. Washington and the opportunity offered there to get an education. I at once applied for admission. I received a letter from the Principal admitting me to school in the autumn of 1889, when I was twenty-two years of age. I did not enter the school, however, until 1890. I registered as a night-school student and asked to be assigned to the carpenter-shop, as that seemed more in line with coopering. This division was so crowded that I was forced to take shoemaking instead. At this trade I worked two years and attended night-school. At the end of this period I resolved to go to North Alabama and work in the coal-mines to get money for clothing, books, and to help me along with my expenses when the money earned at Tuskegee should run out. Realizing that every dollar in my school life would count, I decided to live most cheaply, even cooking for myself. In the end, following this method, I had more money with which to return to school. I worked all day and returned to work again the same night, that I might not lose the prize of education, the pursuit of which I kept daily before me.

Somewhere I heard this quotation, "If anybody else can, I can, too." With this sentiment I continued to push ahead, until in May, 1895, I completed the course of study with the first honor of my class.

During my stay at Tuskegee I made such a record in the shoemaking-shop that my instructor was anxious to have me take an assistant's place with him. This I refused, preferring to start a career in Texas, of which I had heard such glowing accounts. In the months of June, July, and a

EVOLUTION OF A SHOEMAKER

part of August, 1895, I was employed with others making the shoes which constituted a part of Tuskegee's Industrial Exhibit at the Atlanta Exposition. At the solicitation of a number of persons living at Mineola, Tex., I decided, even before graduation, to begin my life-work at that place. Reaching Mineola, I found a fight on hand between the teacher of the colored school and the patrons of the school. Immediately on learning this fact I withdrew from the contest, notwithstanding the fact that my cash earnings were almost exhausted and those who had invited me there seemed unable to guarantee me the position. An incident occurred at Mineola which I shall never forget. It was the second meeting with Prof. H. T. Kealing, then president of Paul Quinn College, Waco, Tex., but now editor of the African Methodist Episcopal Church Review, an ambitious magazine publication of the great African Methodist Episcopal Church. The occasion was a Quarterly Conference of the African Methodist Episcopal Church at Mineola, and Professor Kealing was there to deliver a lecture. Our first meeting was at Tuskegee while I was a student there during my Senior year. In that far-away country I was very glad to see some one I knew, and after the meeting I was not long in making myself known to Professor Kealing. He heard my story, praised the stand I had taken, and expressed regrets that he was not able to offer me a place in Paul Quinn College. He suggested that I take a letter of introduction to Dr. I. B. Scott, then president of Wiley University, Marshall, Tex., but now a Bishop in the Methodist Episcopal Church, the first colored man to be elected to the episcopacy of that great church.

At Wiley I was kindly received by Bishop Scott, and entered into a contract with him to teach shoemaking for my board and the proceeds of the shop. I entered into the spirit of Wiley with such earnestness that at the close of my first month I was made a salaried teacher at $35 a month, and before the session was half gone my salary had been raised to $40. I completed the year's work with perfect satisfaction to all concerned. What I enjoyed most of all during my year at Wiley was the esteem and personal friendship of Bishop Scott. His letters addressed to me upon the eve of my resignation, the esteem he placed on my work while in the employ of the University, and his entreaties that I should not tender my resignation so embarrassed me that for

EVOLUTION OF A SHOEMAKER

a time I was unable to tell what I should do. I felt I owed it to Tuskegee to go wherever Principal Washington thought my services were most desired. On two occasions since I left there Bishop Scott has taken occasion to voice his approval of my conduct while at Wiley: once before the East Tennessee Conference of the Methodist Episcopal Church, and in October, 1902, to my students, when he came to visit me at the Christiansburg Institute.

About the first of May, 1896, I received a telegram from Principal Washington requesting me to allow him to present my name to the Board of Managers of the Christiansburg Industrial Institute for the principalship then vacant. I agreed, and was elected to the place. Before entering upon the duties of my new position at Christiansburg I made a visit to Tuskegee, for the purpose of gaining information as to the scope of my work and as to how I should best proceed.

After spending nearly two months at Tuskegee, I made my way to my new field of labor in Virginia, reaching Christiansburg the 15th of July, 1896. The appearance of things at Christiansburg did not come up to my expectations, nor was my reception in accordance with what I had expected. Under the conditions which then existed, one of more experience than I had would have expected just about such a reception as I received. The people seemed almost crazed that a Tuskegee graduate should be planning to engraft the Tuskegee Idea in that section—and this, too, in spite of Hampton. In my effort to carry out the plans sanctioned by Dr. Washington, I soon realized I was facing opposition well-nigh insurmountable. This was due to their misunderstanding of Dr. Washington, and of what Tuskegee really stands for. As far as possible, I gathered around me men and women who, like myself, were thoroughly imbued with the Tuskegee Idea, and together we pushed ahead with our plans.

From the first I was given to understand that the desire of the Board was that there should be at Christiansburg a school similar to Hampton and Tuskegee; though smaller, it should be no less perfect in what it was designed to do. To reach this end the school had to undergo the change from a distinctly literary school to one with both literary and industrial branches; from a regular, ordinary school to one with a boarding department. My plans met the approval of all concerned, yet there was little idea on my part as to the amount of

GIRLS GARDENING.

EVOLUTION OF A SHOEMAKER

money and labor necessary to put them into operation. The course of study was rearranged to suit the new conditions, and five industries were installed. A circular setting forth the purposes of the school was published and scattered abroad. We then thought that this was nearing the end of the great task, when in reality we had hardly begun.

The Board of Managers did not oppose the boarding department, yet they did not sanction it to the extent of supporting it.

I had confidence in my plans and was willing to start alone. This step was far more perplexing than I had at first imagined. As the time drew near for the opening of school, I was aware that for the boarding department I had to find a suitable house and procure necessary furniture. In the basement of the school building was some lumber which had been used for a platform. With the assistance of one of the teachers this stage-lumber was converted into five bedsteads and three small tables. I succeeded in getting one of the merchants to credit us for several lamps. With this furniture, several stools, an equal number of dry-goods boxes, and a few kitchen utensils, the boarding department of the institution was started. Notwithstanding the scanty arrangement, I am glad to say that for the most part there was but little or no complaint.

Sufficient money was appropriated by the Board of Managers to provide for the purchase of necessary working tools for the added industrial classes.

I kept our friends in the North reminded of our need of additional land. The industrial-school idea with a department of agriculture was not succeeding well on a half-acre of ground. After two years of patient toil this question of land was recognized as a necessity, and accordingly two friends undertook to solicit subscriptions to the amount of $5,000 with which to purchase a farm of 100 acres, two horses, a set of harness, a wagon, and a plow. By this time spring was well on and we were planning to make a crop. In a runaway one of the school horses was badly injured. The purchase of the farm, etc., had about exhausted our Northern resources and the school was in debt. To my credit in the Bank of Christiansburg was a small sum of money, with which I purchased a horse. The crop that year was fairly successful.

Before taking possession of the farm, it was understood that instead of the proceeds of the

EVOLUTION OF A SHOEMAKER

farm going toward maintaining or paying teachers' salaries, the money should go toward building up the soil, which was well run down, and that we should devote all possible effort in the direction of restoring the soil to its once high state of fertilization. Owning this farm, we had the "Big House" where the master once lived, and several of the slave cabins, which still remain, where the slaves resided. Hundreds of slaves, I have been told, tilled this soil in the days long ago, when its productive power was greater than that of any estate in this whole section.

It is a remarkable and significant fact that where the master once lived is a recitation building for colored boys and girls, and where the slaves once huddled around the flickering light of a pine-knot young Negro students are quartered daily, preparing for the duties of the morrow.

In building up the school to its present position, five persons, almost from the very beginning, have figured most prominently, viz.: E. A. Long and his wife, Miss Willie Mae Griffin, the writer and his wife—all Tuskegee graduates. It is needless that I remark here that the burdens borne by the men have been in no sense heavier than those borne by these faithful women. The road along which we have traveled has not been, by any means, a smooth one. We all had been toilers at Tuskegee and knew well how to face the duties of life. This was decidedly in our favor. I was the oldest of the company and perhaps had seen more of hardship than the others; it therefore fell to my lot to give courage to the others when hope was all but gone.

Some time previous to our taking possession of the farm, some of the occupants had sown about half an acre in a kind of radish commonly known hereabout as "pig radish." It must be remembered that each year, after the eight months' academic work was over, we received no money from any source whatever. Paying the salaries of teachers who were to leave for the summer and meeting other demands of the institution always exhausted the school's treasury before the summer season began. With a "cropping" season of four months ahead, no money, no source from which any could be expected, the nice tender "pig radish," year after year, became our food-supply for the early part of the summer at least. Thus, while pushing the operations of the farm, rebuilding the soil by means of turning under green crops, fertilizers, etc., "pig-radish" greens, western side

EVOLUTION OF A SHOEMAKER

meat, and corn-meal constituted our chief diet. Beef came to us as a luxury twice a week. The work was divided so that E. A. Long, our treasurer, was gardener, I was farmer, our wives and Miss Griffin were matrons and cooks. The 4th of July, 1900, found the work of the farm in such a prosperous condition that it was decided to celebrate the event with a cake and some ice-cream, for by this time we owned a cow.

One peculiar thing happened about the time we purchased this farm. We were teaching a graded school which we were eager to turn into a boarding institution. The pupils and patrons were in perfect accord with the faculty, but as soon as the fact became known that we had purchased a large tract of land and would endeavor to build a boarding and industrial school thereon, the members of the faculty at once became objects of scorn to almost the entire colored population. There were at that time enrolled in the school 240 children. Within less than a month more than 100 had dropped out. When school closed in May there were only 60 children attending.

We went about our duties, however, without complaint. While we worked, Nature also worked for us. Vegetation flourished wherever seed were sown; the trees bore a harvest of apples such as I have not seen since, and all went well.

As I look back over those years of trial, of privation, of sacrifice, I find they were conditions precedent to laying an enduring foundation. Our hope has been to establish a school where poor but earnest boys and girls can secure an education. It was through our efforts, first of all, that we were able to prove to the supporters of the school that such an institution could live and grow and do great and lasting good for those it is designed to help. Year by year the school has grown. Year by year the people of the community realize the sincerity of my teachers and give them hearty support. Patience, toil, trust in God, and enterprise are the elements which are fast putting this work on its feet.

Every person who visits the school sees earnestness manifested on farm, in shop, in class, about the grounds, everywhere, and goes away a sincere friend. Not alone do we have our visitor's friendship, but he tells the simple story to others and the number of friends increases.

Mr. R. C. Bedford, of Beloit, Wis., after visiting the school in January, 1905, took occasion to address a gentleman in the North who had interested himself in raising funds for the school, in the

EVOLUTION OF A SHOEMAKER

following language: " I have not visited the school for three years. Great changes have taken place since then. The good there being accomplished is simply immeasurable. Mr. Marshall and Mr. Long work together in such perfect harmony as to constitute a force of singular directness and power. I think the work is carried on most economically, and such a clear and full account of all expenditures is given to the public that you must have the utmost confidence of all your friends."

A few years ago it was difficult for our Treasurer to raise $1,875. The raising of funds for institutions is always difficult, but it is not as hard now to raise $6,000 to $8,000 as it was to raise $1,875 a few years ago.

Mr. E. A. Long, our treasurer, whose faithful assistance I have had in every effort to develop the school, was with me, embarrassed by a debt of the boarding department of more than $600. This condition grew, in a large measure, out of the fact that we attempted to supply students' work on the farm to pay their expenses, and the proceeds of the farm were expended as far as possible in the direction of building up the soil. In the fall of 1902 the board of managers assumed the responsibility of the boarding department, paid all indebtedness, and to-day the school is operated on a cash basis.

During four years there have been contributed toward this work $43,528.77. We have added to the original plant one $10,000 dormitory, a cottage costing $750, a barn at a cost of $2,000, and a shop building valued at $1,000. Much has been spent in the way of repairs. We have $1,000 invested in live stock, and more than $300 worth of farming implements. In each of the industrial departments fairly good equipment can be found. We have grown from a half acre of ground to more than 100 acres; from 2 horses to 43 head of live stock; from a printing-press weighing 75 pounds to one weighing 2,500 pounds. Agriculture, carpentry, printing, shoemaking, laundering, cooking, sewing, and basketry are carried on successfully. The farm produces large crops of cereals, vegetables, fruits, and raises a large share of the meat used by the school. All the flour for the past three years came from the wheat produced on the farm.

The growth of the school has commended itself favorably to those who have had occasion to investigate its claims. A committee appointed to look into the condition of the school some time ago

EVOLUTION OF A SHOEMAKER

made the following statement: "In conclusion, your committee would say that it feels that Messrs. Marshall and Long and their wives have made many sacrifices for the good of the school and have shown a true missionary spirit in carrying on the work, and their ideals and purposes are in accord with the very best. They have borne an awkward and heavy burden in financing the school, and your committee feels that if released from this care their teaching-work will be much improved and become very valuable in building up the school."

In addition to the cultivation of the home-farm of 100 acres, the increased amount of stock makes it necessary to rent an adjacent pasture of 80 acres, the property of two of our teachers.

I have made an effort to supplement the knowledge acquired at Tuskegee through a school of correspondence and through the Chautauqua Reading Circle with some degree of success.

The success of this school, in a very large measure, is due to the consecrated effort of the members of the Friends' Freedmen's Association of Philadelphia and the board of managers of the institution. From the time I entered upon the work to the present, Principal Washington has also been a constant source of help and encouragement. Five hundred dollars given by him in the spring of 1903 was the first money toward the erection of our new dormitory. A combination woodworking-machine is also a result of his interest.

We have on hand an endowment fund of several thousand dollars which we are anxious to increase. Definite plans have been made for the erection of two new buildings. When the plans thus far mapped out are completed, the plant, now worth $30,000, will easily have a valuation of $75,000.

(1)

THE END

Waynesburg College Library
Waynesburg, Pa. 15370